The History of Wales

History Nerds

Published by History Nerds, 2022.

THE HISTORY OF WALES

First edition. August 22, 2022.

Copyright © 2022 History Nerds.

ISBN: 979-8215985700

Written by History Nerds.

Also by History Nerds

Celtic History
Ireland

Great Wars of the World
World War 1
World War 2
The Napoleonic Wars: One Shot at Glory
The Serbian Revolution: 1804-1835
Peace Won by the Saber: The Crimean War, 1853-1856
The Wars of the Roses

Irish Heroes
Grace O'Malley: The Pirate Queen of Ireland
William Butler Yeats: Nobel Prize Winning Poet
Scáthach
Finn McCool

The History of the Vikings

Vikings
Longships on Restless Seas

The Rise and Fall of Empires
Rome: The Rise and Fall

Standalone
The History of the United Kingdom
The History of Ireland
The History of America
Stalin
The Fiery Maelstrom of Freedom
The History of Scotland
Robert the Bruce
William Wallace: Scotland's Great Freedom Fighter
The History of Wales

Table of Contents

Introduction

Much can be said for a nation as proud and ancient as Wales. It is a nation that reaches far back into the shadows of history, from where it struggled to retain its freedom and proud culture. Of Celtic and Brittonic origins, the Welsh people were always fighting fiercely to protect their land's boundaries and preserve their heritage, language, and customs. It is from that fight that a proud sovereign nation emerged, now a respected part of the United Kingdom. Through centuries and ups and downs, this nation left behind a fantastic historic record giving us a lot to explore and write about. In the pages of this book, we will retrace the steps of the Welsh, from the dark ages of Stone and Bronze, through the tumultuous times of the Romans and Anglo-Saxons, on through the fierce Middle Ages, and ultimately the flight into the near-modern times. Perhaps rightly called the "last of the Britons," the modern Welsh people are proud of their ancient Celtic origins, which they preserved even in the face of conquests and attacks from invaders. We will explore this ancient heritage and closely examine the sources of the modern-day Welsh people, their unique language, and their connections with other modern Celtic nations.

Chapter I

Today, we can retrace the evidence of human habitation in Wales through archeology, which has yielded considerable evidence in the excavations of caves and shelters. Some of these caves are the Cae-Gwyn cave near the town of St. Asaph, the Cat's Hole in West Dyfed, Coygan in southern Dyfed, and Paviland in Gower. Archeological evidence suggests the early inhabitants ate oxen, reindeer, and other similar wild animals, primarily depending on the region of their habitation. The tools of the time were made from stone, roughly chiseled and chipped, crude in their construction.

Nevertheless, the more we get nearer in time, the more considerable evidence of the earliest people in Wales we can spot. One of the most famous archeological sites showing evidence of human occupation in early Neolithic times is the so-called "Goat's Hole" site, situated in Paviland in Gower. Proudly called one of the oldest human dwelling places and tombs in Wales, this cave site yielded many stone tools. More importantly, a buried headless skeleton of a young man was discovered at the site that was ritually buried long before our present day. Today, the cave is situated on the coast, but at the time of the burial, it would have been located approximately 110 km (70 miles) inland, overlooking a plain. The skeleton shows us a good insight into the customs of early man: it was stained entirely with red ochre and buried with grave goods such as Periwinkle shells. Upon its discovery in 1823, the excavator, William Buckland, wrote:

"I found the skeleton enveloped by a coating of a kind of ruddle ... which stained the earth, and in some parts extended itself to the distance of about half an inch [12 mm] around the surface of the bones ... Close to that part of the thigh bone where the pocket is usually worn surrounded also by ruddle [were] about two handfuls of the Nerita littoralis [periwinkle shells]. At another part of the skeleton, viz in contact with the ribs [were] forty or fifty fragments of ivory rods [also] some small

*fragments of rings made of the same ivory and found with the rods ...
Both rods and rings, as well as the Nerite shells, were stained superficially
with red, and lay in the same red substance that enveloped the bones."*

From this unique account and astonishing discovery, we can take a good look into the regional customs of Wales' earliest inhabitants. The funerary tradition of dying the deceased with red ochre has been recorded elsewhere in Europe, and it can be safely assumed that the custom traveled as far west as Wales. Let us remind ourselves that the English Channel was at the time a fertile, spacious plain known now as Doggerland. It would not be impossible for hunter-gatherer nomads to journey westwards in their pursuit of wild game and have reached the bountiful land now in Wales. Perhaps the skeleton from Paviland was one such nomad. This find is considered the oldest dated ceremonial burial in Western Europe.

Of course, as time went on, the hunter-gatherer lifestyle slowly gave way to a sedentary lifestyle, i.e., a communal life of villages, towns, and walled communities. People slowly began unraveling the mysteries of agriculture and animal husbandry as new technologies, but also of warfare and tribal affiliations. As the ages passed, so did new migrants and new nomads arrived in Wales, all leaving their marks on the region. Between 6,500 BC and 6,200 BC, that fertile plain of Doggerland, connecting the British Isles with mainland Europe, was finally submerged beneath the frigid seas due to rising sea levels. This eventually separated the British Isles from the rest of Europe, just as it is today. It was around this time that a new wave of migrants arrived. The Mesolithic (or Middle Stone Age) folk had already spread over Europe; however, in Wales, their culture remained in its primitive stages, again having no chance to fulfill its most significant potential. A greater inclination towards sedentary life characterized the Mesolithic age. Evidence shows that these people fished on the shores and hunted game on the edges of the great forests that dotted the region. Their weapons, made from stone, bone, and flint, were simple but not crude.

Again, the population of Wales was relatively minuscule, never exceeding a few thousand at most.

The Neolithic Age, however, brought new and increasing changes to the societies across Europe. The significant change that the Neolithic brought was begun in the Middle East, roughly around 9,000 BC. The Fertile Crescent was always the ground from which new changes sprung. Advanced cultivation methods appeared, as did the domestication of animals, better known as *animal husbandry*. These recent "trends" and technologies from the Middle East gradually spread westwards into Europe through trade and migrations. However, they would take a little longer to reach the British Isles, Wales. The most significant route for spreading this technology was through the Mediterranean basin, across the Western seas, and along the coasts of Atlantic Europe. The Neolithic age thus reached the area of Wales perhaps around 4,000 to 3,000 BC. This marks the beginning of the Neolithic Age in Wales. Archeological excavations yielded improved stone axes and tools, adopting the practice of herding animals and some of the first land cultivation in Wales. Also appearing around this time are the enigmatic Megalithic burial practices that would become iconic across Europe and in the British Isles. Great chambered tombs were constructed, especially of the *cromlech* and *dolmen* type, and most certainly reserved for the most powerful and respected members of these ancient societies. As this age progressed, the increased social structure appeared, and fragments of an early and widespread "Paleo European" culture appeared.

Some of the most notable chambered tombs dated to this time are the famed *Bryn Celli Ddu* and *Barclodiad y Gawres* on Anglesey, the *Llech-y-Filliast* in the Vale of Glamorgan, or the *Pentre Ifan* site in Pembrokeshire. These magnificent megalithic sites are sure evidence of a functioning, close-knit society with a set of beliefs and traditions. Some of these structures defy the laws of logic and likely took a long time to complete. For example, the burial chamber of Llech-y-Filliast, known commonly as Tinkinswood, is topped off by a single great capstone that weighs about 40 tons. Erecting such a monument, and raising that stone, was undoubtedly a communal task and involved dozens, if not hundreds, of individuals. That is an excellent example of a functioning society and some ancient teamwork. Once completed, however, these burial chambers were used across generations, perhaps for hundreds of years. At Tinkinswood, the bones of around fifty persons were unearthed and buried across generations. The accompanying pottery shards were similar in style to those made in southern England at the time.

Did You Know?

The oldest living bird in 2008 was actually from Wales! It was a Manx Shearwater, living on Bardsey Island in Wales. It was ringed (tagged) in 1957 and likely born in 1952; it has been believed to have traveled more than 5 million miles. It is interesting to know that more than half of the world's population of Manx Shearwaters lives in Wales, on the islands of Bardsey, Skokholm, and Skomer. With nearly 200,000 nesting pairs on these islands collectively, Wales boasts the highest concentration of these birds worldwide.

Some Neolithic communities across the British Isles erected specific oblong houses and similar dwellings with unique ridge roofs carried on rows of upright posts. Such examples have been excavated at Newton Nottage near Porthcawl and Clegyr Boia near St. David's, amongst others. However, a lot remains unknown about the buildings of the time since material such as wood does not survive for so long in standard conditions. Much of what once existed had wholly disappeared since. Life in caves was still commonplace, as it was efficient, provided ample protection, and required almost no effort. Others, however, lived in open settlements of a primitive type, on spurs of land near the coast. At the time, certain parts of Wales were the regional centers of the production of stone tools. As we said, new technologies were slower in reaching this far west, and the use of metals (i.e., the Copper and the Bronze Ages) appeared later than in other parts of Europe.

Nevertheless, ancient inhabitants of Wales mastered the use of stone and the production of stone tools. Tools dated to this period are exceptionally made, polished to a high standard, and made from the highly durable igneous rock in abundant supply in Wales. In June 1919, an archeological excavation in Penmaenmawr in the north of Gwynedd uncovered a late Neolithic ax "factory." Stone axes from this site have been found as far as Wiltshire, north Ireland, and south Scotland. This is crucial evidence of developed trade and social networks. Both these, and the remnants of the magnificent passage tombs, are a mute witness to the rich prehistory of Wales and the British Isles.

However, these ancient times were, as we said, marked by frequent migrations of newly emerging cultures, new people, and civilizations. Sometimes, it was merely influence that journeyed across the land; cultural traits exchanged through trade and contact. At other times, people sailed and traveled in search of new lands to settle, better prospects, and riches. Around 2,500 to 2,000BC, the Beaker Folk arrived in parts of Wales. These were the carriers of the Bronze Age culture, well known for their distinctive burial practices, where they'd cremate their dead and place their ashes into earthen urns. Some evidence suggests that these people sailed from the Iberian Peninsula and sought better prospects across the sea in Wales. Roughly 30 of these burials have been discovered in Wales, mostly reserved for coastal plains in the south and the north, areas best reached from the sea; or in the valleys of the Severn, Usk, or Wye, best accessed from the east.

Either way, this is good evidence that the Beaker Folk migrations failed to reach the western highlands of Wales, where the original Neolithic inhabitants continued to thrive. Either way, the arrival of the Beaker Folk brought into Wales the art of bronze-working.

The first metal tools in Wales were found around 2,500 BC, initially made from copper and only later from bronze. Great mines associated with the Bronze industry have been discovered in Wales, making it a regional hotspot for trade goods. Most of the copper needed to produce bronze was likely taken from the Great Orme copper mine, where large-scale mining dates to the middle Bronze Age. Of course, with the introduction of the Bronze Age and the arrival of new cultures, the landscape of ancient Wales became transformed. Gone for good are the ancient ways of the nomads, the hunters and gatherers, and the matriarchal societies of Old Europe. In a patriarchal society where riches and power ruled over men, war was on the menu. The earliest hillforts, significant fortified settlements, first appeared during this period, likely due to the rise of regional chieftains, who fought one another over money, wealth, and ore. The noted Welsh historian John Davies offered a theory that it was not only the material goods that gave rise to hillforts but also a worsening climate.

After 1250 BC, lower temperatures and heavier rainfall resulting from climate change likely required the best areas of productive land to be defended. This was a significant turn for the worse after the dry and mild climate that dominated the early Bronze Age. Towards the beginning of the first millennium BC, the weather worsened: heavy rain and strong winds deteriorated the soil and the crops, deforestation was alarming, and the once-fertile upland farms were quickly deserted. All this contributed significantly to the significant socio-economic changes in ancient Wales, creating a volatile mood amongst its inhabitants. It would seem that a sudden and urgent need for economic and military security arose, resulting in the numerous hillforts being constructed, today major relics of prehistoric times. Around 600 such fortified settlements have been identified in Wales alone, which is a considerable number. Harsh times created harsh men, and simple farming communities had to rely on protecting the fortified walls. Cattle thieves and roving warriors roamed the land, and the vulnerable folk flocked to these formidable defensive positions on top of hills and other strategic places. Today, the largest and most complex of these fortified settlements are visible at Llanymynech, Breiddin, and Ffridd Faldwyn.

The Bronze Age gradually gave way to the Iron Age, somewhat sooner in Wales than in other parts of Europe. In the Iron Age, we can see the faint outlines of the Welsh identity, the unique and distinct Brittonic nation forming out of a tumultuous era. The earliest documented iron implements discovered in Wales come from Llyn Fawr reservoir, situated at the head of the Rhondda Valley. Several artifacts were uncovered: an iron sword, spearhead, and sickle. The small "hoard" was likely deposited as a form of votive offering, a common tradition of the ancient world. Archeologists dated these iron items to roughly 650 BC; some of them, such as the sickle, display traces of local production. During the Iron Age, building hillforts continued in earnest and on a grander scale. Some of the most prominent from this age are located at Pen Dinas near Aberystwyth and Tre'r Ceiri on the Llŷn Peninsula. The earliest positively dated Iron Age settlement in Wales is also located on Llŷn Peninsula, at Castell Odo's site, dated around 400 BC.

However, one of Wales's most significant Iron Age finds was discovered between 1942 and 1943 at Llyn Cerrig Bach on Anglesey. It was an accidental discovery while constructing a Royal Air Force base. Workers uncovered a massive cache that contained weapons, shields, chariots (with their fittings and harnesses), slave chains, and tools. Many of those had been broken deliberately, indicating a massive votive offering. This cache of items gives us a glimpse into an essential part of the history of Wales, its Celtic identity. The find is considered one of

Britain's most critical La Tène metalwork collections. We already know that the La Tène culture is associated with the Celts.

We can see that at one point in history, the region of modern-day Wales adopted a Celtic culture, language, identity, and traditions. When and how this exactly happened can never be said with certainty because of the great extent of the Celtic culture and the complexity of its origins. However, it can be safely assumed that the Celtic language was spoken in Wales by about 700 BC. Until recently, scholars held that the Celtic culture was spread westwards across Europe towards the British Isles using a large-scale invasion. Remember, the Irish, Manx, Cornish, and Scottish are also Celtic cultures. However, this view is no longer credible, and it is most likely that the Celtic language and culture were spread by cultural diffusion through trade, economy, small-scale migrations, and movements of people. After all, the earliest forms of the Celtic culture, and later its La Tène and Hallstatt variations, spread throughout most of Europe and influenced varied ethnic groups. It was the "trend," so to speak, the lingua franca of ancient Europe, the language of trade and aristocracy, and little could stop its fast spread.

Even the name of Wales is Celtic in origins, as, of course, the Welsh language is from the Celtic family. It is a relic of a time when Wales was just a part of a larger entity, the great land of the Britons. For example, the Welsh endonym (their name for themselves), *Cymry*. This is a word descended from the Brythonic word *kombrogi*, which means "fellow countrymen," i.e., "kinsmen, brethren," etc. It is an authentic relic of an ancient era when Britain was the home of a singular people with one language and a shared, Brythonic Celtic culture. Of course, we cannot confidently say that this name was used in ancient times. It is much more likely that the endonym "Cymry" came into use sometime in the 6th or 7th century AD, in the early middle ages, when a need arose in Post-Roman Britain for a strong relationship with other Brythonic-speaking peoples, especially those living in northern

England and Southern Scotland, in the ancient realm of *Yr Hen Ogledd,* or the "Old North." There also existed an older, more generic, and literary term of *Brythoniaid,* which was used more to describe any of the Brythonic peoples, Welsh included. However, after 1100 AD, this term fell out of favor, and Cymry remained the dominant designation for the Welsh.

You may ask, what about that latter term, the Welsh? You should not be surprised that it is not Celtic in origin but Anglo-Saxon! The original word is "wealh," stemming from the Proto-Germanic word "Walhaz," derived from the name of the Gaulish people known to the Romans as Volcae. It was used in Germanic languages as a way to refer indiscriminately to all inhabitants of the Roman Empire. When the Old English-speaking Anglo-Saxons arrived in the British Isles, they used that exact term for the Britons they encountered. As the Britons were subjugated and assimilated step by step, and their territories became smaller, the plural of the word Wealh, *Wēalas,* ended up being used for the last genuinely Brythonic, pre-Anglo-Saxon land, Wales. Interestingly, we can spot a similar word origin for modern names of some Romance-speaking peoples in Continental Europe, Wallonia, Wallachia, Valais, Vlachs, Włochy, and so on.

Did You Know?

The village of Goldcliff, on the shores of southern Wales near Newport, has a vibrant history. Here, the land has been continually reclaimed from the sea, and the area is famed for its glittering cliffs and drainage ditches. The Roman-era Goldcliff stone was discovered, which records the work of legionaries who built an ancient sea wall. The stone reads: "The Century of Statorius Maximus in the 1st Cohort, built thirty-one and a half paces". This, however, is not the earliest piece of history of this region. In the laminated silts of the Severn Estuary foreshore at Goldcliff are hidden 8,000-year-old human footprints dated to the Mesolithic. They were shown on the TV Show Time Team and are an important glimpse into the ancient history of Wales. In 1113 AD, the Goldcliff Priory was established. The earliest drainage ditches were still called "Monksditch." In 1188 AD, Giraldus Cambrensis writes of the small cliffs at "Gouldclyff," which are "glittering with a wonderful brightness." Indeed, even today, when the sun is shining, it hits a bed of yellow mica stone, and reflects glittering light to the passing ship, giving a beautiful display, and Goldcliff its name.

To return for a moment to the Welsh endonym, Cymry. To find a similar term amongst the Brythonic Celts, we look for languages closest to Welsh. In this case, that would be Cornish and Breton, both sharing similarities with Welsh since they are from the same family and have the same origins. Remember, the Bretons we refer to here are the Celtic minority of modern-day France, living in Bretagne or Brittany. These Celts were always just a stone's throw from Cornwall and Wales, across the channel, and shared cultural links and traditions are well attested. However, there are no counterparts to the word "Cymry" in either Cornish or Breton. Still, let's look at the medieval Irish manuscript, the "Sanas Cormaic," or "Cormac's Glossary," written around 900 AD, where the language is called "Combrec" and is named the tongue of the Britons. We can see no distinction between Combrec, Bretnas, or Welsh and Breton. We can thus understand that they were seen as varieties of the same language, spoken in Cornwall, Wales, and Brittany. We can also spot the same root in the name of Cumberland and the ancient Cumbrians; that root is *combrogi* or *kombrogi*, i.e., "fellow countrymen."

Chapter II

The Iron Age in Wales is the Celtic Age. A lot has been said about the Celts, as they arose to become perhaps the most dominant civilization in Iron Age Europe. By 500 BC, they were much more than a unified, recognizable people. Even though they never managed to establish a vast kingdom or a unified empire, they spread across Europe, and their expansion was extraordinary. The Celts grew to become the main enemies of the Romans. The latter mockingly dubbed them the "barbarians," but it was these barbarians that sacked Rome and the sacred temples of Delphi. Their vast territories stretched from Ireland in the west to Galatia in modern-day Turkey to the east. And it is no secret that the Romans greatly feared the Celts. These were a warlike people, much in the vein of their forebears, the Indo-Europeans. They were fiercely bold, devoted to combat, and proud of their unique two-wheeled chariots. They fought naked, with spears and longswords, and made a tradition of beheading their enemies. Their prowess in warfare was well-attested, as was their fearsome appearance: they were tall, well-built, fair-skinned, and had blue eyes, but war was not their only mastery.

The Celts were renowned for their masterful art. They were skilled metalworkers, architects, and craftsmen. Celtic art was highly sought after, and its intricacy was unparalleled in the ancient world. This art originated in the Celtic core lands at La Tene and Hallstatt. The former was particularly striking and awe-inspiring. It boasted abstract and complex geometric designs, full of swirls, plant and oriental motifs, intricately displayed on swords, daggers, brooches, bracelets, shields, pins, rings, and firedogs. Many have called it the genius of Celtic art, and that genius and culture gradually found their way to Wales. As we said, scholars have shifted from the archaic theory that stated that the Celtic culture arrived in Wales through a large-scale invasion and some mythical massive migration of peoples. It simply did not work that way. The accepted theory states that this culture arrived in the region through cultural diffusion across the seaways and trade. It likely took more than a thousand years for the Celtic language and culture to replace prehistoric civilization fully. Even a change that takes thousands of years can be undone in just a few generations. That undoing is the arrival of the Romans.

Before the arrival of the Romans, the Celts in Wales lived separated into several tribes. As is traditional for this culture, most of these tribes were at war with one another. One of the main flaws of the Celtic civilization was a lack of unity that prevented them from accomplishing more extraordinary deeds. As a consequence, the area of Wales lacked social and political agreement, which paved the way for a relatively easy Roman conquest. Moreover, the north and south of Wales had significant cultural differences, with the latter being more in tune with the rest of Britain and the former remaining more conservative and slower to progress. Nevertheless, the entirety of Wales was pretty much left to itself, and it saw little outside influence from the rest of Britain until the arrival of the Romans.

In August 55 BC, the famed Julius Caesar landed on the coasts of Kent with 10,000 soldiers at his back. At the time, he was knee-deep in his notorious conquest of Gaul, the Celtic land in today's France. However, his ambitions and vague excuses for punitive operations led him to cross the Channel and see for himself what lay in these lands of Britons. However, Caesar's landing was merely a survey; the Romans did not return to Britain until after a century had passed. During their absence, the Britons thrived in their usual manner. A prosperous kingdom was on the rise in Essex and Surrey, led by one Cunobelinus of the Catuvellauni tribe, known in Welsh tradition as Cynfelyn. His realm created coinage, wheel pottery industry, prosperous agriculture, and flourishing trade. Around his empire were tribes of Dubonni, Coritani, and Iceni, and beyond them the land of modern Wales, with its inhabitants, the tribes of Silures, Demetae, Ordovices, and

Deceangli. The shadow of Rome spread across Europe and could not be avoided. After the powerful King Cunobelinus died, one of his exiled sons fled to the Romans, seeking their aid to recover his lands. It was an excuse the Romans needed to set foot in Britain and finally conquer it. A planned campaign by Emperor Caligula never came to fruition, but the latter one by Emperor Claudius was a success. Betraying those who sought its help, Rome quickly jumped at the chance to expand its borders and seize the fertile lowlands of Britain. The conquest of Britain began in earnest around 43 AD and was primarily completed in the south by 87 AD. In just over 40 years, the Romans swept across the British tribes, placing them under their control. However, they had troubles with the Picts and the Scots to the north and could never fully seize their realm.

Of course, the region of Wales and its tribes was conquered alongside the rest of Britain. Still, the lands were taken step by step, and the invasion of Wales was a separate affair. Before it was invaded, the Roman authority in Britain was in the hands of Governor Aulus Plautius, the man who began the conquest of Britain in the name of the Emperor. The Romans had control of all southeastern Britain and Dumnonia, and perhaps even the lowland English Midlands, as far as the River Dee Estuary and the River Mersey. Brigantes were subdued and in agreement with the Romans, as were most other tribes of southeastern Britain. The way was open for the Roman subjugation of the tribes of Wales. However, the lack of contemporary documents leaves much to be pieced together about this time of Welsh history. We know Anglesey was conquered in 60 AD, but what chain of events led to that? We simply don't know. The only written evidence comes from the Roman historian Tacitus, who mentions a hostile incursion into Roman Britain from a tribe called *Decangi*, identified as the Welsh *Deceangli*. This led to a reaction by the Romans, who campaigned against the Deceangli, most likely in 48 to 49 AD. After this tribe was subjugated, the Romans moved to southeastern Wales and fought against the Silures. This tribe was very fierce, and the Romans had to establish a legionary fortress in the area to wage war on them. The famed Silures and the neighboring Ordovices were led by one Caratacus, a king of Britons who fled from southeastern England. In Welsh, he was known as Caradog. After his tribe of Catuvellauni was subjugated, Caradog fled to Wales and Silures, mounting further resistance against the Romans. After conquering Deceangli of north Wales in 48 AD, the latter built a sizeable legionary fortress near where the city of Gloucester would later be founded, not too far from modern-day Wales. This major fort would be linked with more minor defenses at Clyro, Usk, and similar sites. All this was a way to put continued pressure upon the restless Silures of Wales. Caradog was a valiant freedom fighter and fought against all odds. Tacitus, the Roman historian, wrote a lot about the invasion of Britain and mentioned Caradog on several occasions. The fight against him was carried out by one Publius Ostorius Scapula, the successor of governor Aulus Plautius. The latter finally caught up with Caradog and his army in 50 AD, defeating him in one final decisive battle. Today we do not know the exact site of that battle, except that it was within the territory of the Ordovices tribe. Tacitus writes:

"The army then marched against the Silures, a naturally fierce people and now full of confidence in the might of Caratacus, who by many an indecisive and many a successful battle had raised himself far above all the other generals of the Britons. Inferior in military strength but deriving an advantage from the deceptiveness of the country, he at once shifted the war by a stratagem into the territory of the Ordovices, where, joined by all who dreaded peace with us, he resolved on a final struggle. [Caratacus] selected a position for the engagement in which advance and retreat alike would be difficult for our men and comparatively easy for his own, and then on some lofty hills, wherever their sides could be approached by a gentle slope, he piled up stones to serve as a rampart. A

river too of varying depth was in his front, and his armed bands were drawn up before his defenses."

Alas, the numerically inferior army of Caradog could not match the ferocity of the Roman legions. Ostorius Scapula managed to land a terrible defeat on the Britons, defeating Caradog and effectively subjugating the Silures, nine years after the war began. The loss completely broke the Silures and their fighting ability. Caradog himself managed to escape, but his wife, daughter, and brothers were all captured by the Romans. Caradog fled to the territory of the Brigantes tribe and sought help from their Queen, Cartimandua. However, the latter depended on the Romans for her position and thus betrayed Caradog, imprisoning him and delivering him to the Romans. Caradog's fame and ferocity preceded him by that point, and his fight was well known across the Roman Empire. He was promptly delivered to Rome, where he was to be paraded in a glorious military triumph before all the citizens and the Emperor. As tradition dictated, he was to be killed immediately afterward. Caradog was no ordinary Briton: he was a man with the strength of character who left a strong impression wherever he was. Thus, he got a chance to address none other than the Roman Emperor Claudius. The speech that Caradog delivered left such an immense impression on the Emperor that he decided not to kill him but to free him and make him a citizen of Rome. It was an unprecedented event and one that bears a lot of historicity. Tacitus records his speech as follows:

"When he (Caradog) was set before the emperor's tribunal, he spoke as follows: 'Had my moderation in prosperity been equal to my noble birth and fortune, I should have entered this city as your friend rather than as your captive; and you would not have disdained to receive, under a treaty of peace, a king descended from illustrious ancestors and ruling many nations. My present lot is as glorious to you as it is degrading to myself. I had men and horses, arms and wealth. What wonder if I parted with them reluctantly? If you Romans choose to lord it over the world, does it

follow that the world is to accept slavery? Were I to have been at once delivered up as a prisoner, neither my fall nor your triumph would have become famous. My punishment would be followed by oblivion, whereas, if you save my life, I shall be an everlasting memorial of your clemency.' Upon this, the emperor granted pardon to Caratacus, to his wife, and to his brothers. Released from their bonds, they did homage also to Agrippina who sat near, conspicuous on another throne, in the same language of praise and gratitude."

Even though the leader Caradog was defeated, resistance to Roman rule in Wales did not stop altogether. We learn that the Silures fought on and that two Roman cohorts were defeated around 51 AD, then a legion in 52 AD. In the meantime, the Roman governor for Britain, Publius Ostorius Scapula, died in 52 AD while dealing with all the issues. This gave the Silures a brief moment of respite until a replacement governor would arrive.

Some two years later, Emperor Claudius died in 54 AD and was replaced by the notorious Emperor Nero. Nero's drive and policies were markedly different, ushering in a significant change for the future of Britain. Around 57 AD, Nero authorized a determined campaign that would bring the entirety of Britain under Roman rule. At that time, Britain was governed by a new man, Quintus Veranius, and he began a new campaign of expansion, directed mainly against the Silures. He died soon after, however, and was succeeded by Suetonius Paulinus, who had great success in subjugating northern Wales. By 60 AD, the whole of north Wales was likely under Roman control, as Suetonius set his sights on Anglesey, the primary "stronghold" of the Britons and the center of their powerful Druids. At that point, Anglesey island was the last major strongpoint of the Welsh: it swelled with migrants who fled there and was a major religious center. Many superstitions surrounded Anglesey, and many Roman soldiers feared it in turn. After some initial indecisiveness, the Romans crossed the Menai Strait and assaulted the Welsh army there. The task of crossing the strait fell to the Roman auxiliaries; native Britons were recruited into the Roman army. They knew the crossing points and did not lack courage. Accounts state that they swam over without boats and were naked. Tacitus writes of the assault:

"The skill and resolution of the general accomplished the passage. With some picked men of the auxiliaries, disencumbered of all baggage, who knew the shallows and had that national experience in swimming which enables the Britons to take care not only of themselves but of their arms and horses, he delivered so unexpected an attack that the astonished enemy who was looking for a fleet, a naval armament, and an assault by sea, thought that to such assailants nothing could be formidable or invincible."

So it was that, despite the initial fear and the superstitions, the Romans managed to organize a surprise attack on the Anglesey army and finally subdue the Welsh there. The druids were killed en-masse, their sacred groves and religious places destroyed, and many prisoners taken. It was a significant morale boost for the Romans, but for the Welsh tribes, it was a significant downfall. However, the fates had it different: the Roman victory was short-lived, and they did not get the chance to consolidate their hold on northwest Wales fully. The reason for this was the great rebellion of the Iceni tribe, led by their famed Queen Boudicca, which suddenly erupted in the east and interrupted the Roman consolidation of subjugated Wales. Boudicca's revolt was utterly ferocious and displayed the full wrath of the conquered Britons. Thousands of Romans and their auxiliary allies were slaughtered without mercy. The de facto provincial capital, London, was thoroughly burned down. The Romans responded in equal measure and even harder than that. Tens of thousands of Britons were killed. Norfolk notably was left desolate for generations to come. All this, again, gave a bit of respite to the region of modern Wales and the tribes that dwelt there.

<u>Did You Know?</u>

The famed "Mabinogion" is the greatest treasure of Welsh mythology and folk tales, dating from the eleventh century. They were preserved in the White Book of Rhydderch, between 1300 and 1325 AD, and in the Red Book of Hergest, written around 1400. Many of the legends surrounding King Arthur and his adventures come from these books. Lady Charlotte Guest first translated these tales into English and published them between 1838 and 1849. The stories were divided into three volumes: The Three Romances, The Four Branches of the Mabinogi, and the Four Independent Native Tales. Combined with tales of Taliesin, they are described as "amongst the finest flowerings of Celtic genius, and, taken together, a masterpiece of medieval European literature." The tales of Pwyll', Branwen, Manawyddan, Math, The Dream of Macsen Wledig, Llud and Llefelys, Culhwch and Olwen, and many others, remain one of the essential foundations of Welsh culture and identity.

We need to consider that many events that transpired in Britain under Roman rule were directly affected by events happening elsewhere in the empire, especially in Rome. At the end of the 60s AD, Rome was in great upheaval, ending the Julio-Claudian dynasty. In its place came the Flavian dynasty, established in 69 AD by Emperor Vespasian. Under their reign, the campaigns again picked up the pace. Julius Frontinus was the new governor, and in 74 AD, he continued campaigning against Wales. He prioritized the subjugation of the Silures and the Ordovices, the main Welsh tribes. Just how important and challenging the conquest of Wales can be seen from the fact that the headquarters of three (of the four) legions campaigning in Britain were situated in the borderlands of Wales. From as early as 67 AD, the Twentieth Legion was situated at Viroconium (modern Wroxeter) near Shrewsbury.

In comparison, in 75 AD, a fortress was established for the Second Legion Adiutrix at the banks of the River Dee, at Deva (modern Chester). The third legion stationed there was Second Legion Augusta, stationed at the banks of River Usk at Isca (modern Caerleon). Either way, the campaigns of Frontinus were successful: in 75 AD, he had defeated the Silures for good and extensively wore down the Ordovices. By the end of his term in 77 AD, he managed to subdue most of Wales. His successor, Julius Agricola, completed the task and quelled the Ordovices, and not without great slaughter and bloodshed. Only one tribe of Wales was primarily left intact and undamaged, the Demetae. They chose not to oppose Rome and continued to develop in their lands peacefully, isolated from their neighbors and the Romans. Moreover, the Demetae were the only pre-Roman Welsh tribe to preserve their original tribal name even after the Romans were gone.

Ultimately, the Roman subjugation of Wales proved to be too long and costly. History documents at least thirteen distinct campaigns in Wales and its borders between 48 and 79 AD. There were a lot of contributing factors to the length of this war. The foremost was the scarcity of grain in Wales, the most critical food source for the Roman legions. The second factor was the efficient guerilla warfare of the Welsh tribesmen, who used the mountainous terrain to decimate the invading Romans. It was foremostly the Silures who gave the Romans most trouble. Described as swarthy and stubborn, these fierce warriors were difficult to bend to the will of the Romans. Their ferocious resistance was one of the most significant contributing factors to the protracted Roman campaigns in Wales. Even after the Silures were subdued, as we wrote already, their sporadic resistance continued in parts of Wales. However, by that stage, the Romans were capable of quickly dealing with that threat, thanks to the significant number of legionary forts across the borders of Wales. Caerleon was among the chief Roman forts, stationing a formidable force of around 5,500 heavily armed troopers. It became the headquarters of the Second Augustan Legion in 75 AD and today remains one of the most important Roman military sites in Europe.

Chapter III

Even though the Roman subjugation of Wales proved to be a destructive part of this nation's early history, it nevertheless laid down some pave stones for its later future character. With each passing decade of Roman presence in Britain and Wales, the native Briton inhabitants became gradually "Romanized." Undoubtedly, the first to adopt a Roman character was the ruling, noble members of the native society. In later decades, the Southwest region of Wales became the most Romanized one, and the ruling class of the Silures tribe was quick to adopt the Roman customs. It is proposed that these individuals later founded the Kingdom of Gwent. Another factor that tells us how Roman culture spread across Wales is the country's rich archeological heritage. Numerous sites have been excavated and identified as Roman villas, settlements (*civitates* and *coloniae*), or forts. However, it is worthwhile to note that Roman presence in the country was limited to a great extent by the odd geography of Wales and the lack of fertile and flat agricultural land, on which the Romans depended greatly.

Interestingly, the Romans seem to have accepted certain parts of their conquest. Notably, they did not curb the native Briton religions in their entirety. The noted exception was druidism, which was forbidden and persecuted, as the Romans exceedingly hated and feared the druids and their effect on the native tribes. Other deities, however, were not suppressed. As a result, many of the native, Celtic deities became fused with the Roman ones. We can also see the presence of oriental mystery cults. At Caerleon and Caernarfon, there existed loyal followers of the god Mithraea. However, the most crucial part of this is the very faint, but not to be overlooked, the introduction of Christianity in Wales. At this time, Christianity was still in its infancy in the Roman Empire and was banned and persecuted. Missionaries existed nonetheless and attempted to spread their religion, which was alien in ancient Pagan Europe.

In Wales and across Britain, the initial response to Christianity was hostile. The heathen tribes were not eager to accept a different religion and were not reserved from turning to violence to show that. Some early Christian martyrs in Britain were Aaron and Julius, who were killed in Caerleon around 300 AD because they apparently "disturbed the peace of the gods." However, after the Roman Emperor Constantine became the first ruler to embrace Christianity after 312 AD, this religion was equal to all others that were accepted. Contemporary accounts tell us that by the fourth century AD, small Christian communities conducted regular worship in Wales, especially in the town of Caerwent. Christianity at the time was undoubtedly a certified shortcut to many benefits, as paganism was becoming increasingly demonized and shunned. Christian clergymen were able to learn Latin, the elite language of the empire, and thus were given a "passport" towards influence and wealth. From this time, the first Latin loanwords appeared in the Welsh Brythonic language. Some of the Welsh words that are Latin in origins are *llyfr* (book), *ystafell* (room), and *pont* (bridge), amongst others.

In the end, it is important to emphasize that the extent of the Roman influence in Wales was not all as widespread as it might seem from what we wrote. The degree of Romanization existed, of course. Still, it did not spread so intensely in the remote regions of Wales, outside the heavily militarized zones or rich and thriving cities and urban communities. The Roman footprint was much less visible in the poorer, simpler, remote parts. We can safely say that those people who wore togas, spoke Latin, ate luxuriously, and lived in well-furnished villas were a minority in ancient Wales. Those who adopted Roman ways were guaranteed these benefits, but when the inevitable end of Roman rule came, they would lament it greatly. For decades the Roman withdrawal from Britain was brewing and became an unavoidable certainty.

Contrary to popular belief, the collapse of Roman rule in their British province was not sudden and unexpected. It was a long time coming, and not at all sudden. One of the main reasons for Roman withdrawal from Britain (and Wales) was the increased adverse effect of continuous internal conflicts and unrest within the Empire. A series of Emperors came and went, with few having a stable hold on the throne. Of course, the constant external threats from the so-called "barbarian" tribes that crossed over the empire's boundaries to raid caused this instability. All this was at its height in the fourth century AD. Frankish, Saxon, and Irish raids made it increasingly difficult for the Romans to keep their power in Britain uncontested. The same happened elsewhere in the empire, with various hostile tribes never ceasing to disturb the peace. These great upheavals occurred in the 3rd and 4th centuries AD and shook the ever-fragile foundations of the empire.

Due to the lessened Roman presence in Wales, a different cause existed: the imperial pretensions of Roman generals stationed there. To support their aims for the throne, these generals freely withdrew troops from parts of Britain so they could fight elsewhere. This was made all the more critical when we consider that the presence of Roman soldiers in Wales was the only indication of Roman presence in the land. When the troops that left to remedy issues in other parts of the Empire never returned to Britain, Roman rule was quick to crumble. Even so, it did not end uniformly and appeared in different regions at different times. Villas, towns, and forts were abandoned gradually: Caerwent, for example, was occupied even after the Romans departed, while Carmarthen was slowly abandoned by the late 4th century. Also, there is evidence that Roman customs survived in south Wales as far as the late 5th and early 6th centuries AD. Caerwent was inhabited by Romanized Britons even after all Roman legions were out of the isles. They lived there until at least the early 6th century. There is solid evidence that Early Christianity was established in that town, with the likelihood of a monastery and a bishop existing there.

When touching upon the Roman departure from Britain, we cannot overlook the tradition of Magnus Maximus, who is widely regarded as the "central figure in the emergence of a free Britain in the post-Roman era." Oddly enough, this figure has been firmly rooted in the early origins of the modern Welsh nation, with certain scholars controversially stating that "Wales can be said to begin with the hero Maximus." In legendary Welsh stories, he is cited as the ancestor of kings and saints of that land, and his story is detailed in the *Breuddwyd Macsen Wledig*, the "Dream of Emperor Maximus." The story tells us that he is the Emperor of Rome who marries a wondrous Briton woman and tells her that she can name any desire as a wedding gift. The princess of the Britons asked that her father be given authority over Britain. This suggests that Magnus Maximus (Macsen Wledig) is perhaps the historical figure responsible for transferring the rule back into the hands of native Britons after the Romans departed.

To be sure, Magnus Maximus is a historical figure. He was a Roman of aristocratic birth who rose through the ranks to become a victorious Roman general and won the position of a high-ranking officer in Britain. He got the role in 380 AD and, the following year managed to defeat a force of Picts and Scots. In 383 AD, rising through the ranks, Magnus Maximus went for the biggest prize: the imperial throne. He crossed over from Britain into Gaul, taking a large number of Roman troops with him. In Gaul, he defeated and ousted Emperor Gratian and continued toward Italy. He quickly became emperor of the Western Empire, chiefly Britannia and Gaul, where he minted his coinage. However, his insatiable ambitions led him towards a renewed invasion of Italy, where he had to face Theodosius. In 388 AD, Magnus Maximus was defeated by Theodosius in the Battle of Poetovio and soon after was executed in Aquileia.

When Magnus Maximus departs Britain for Gaul on his campaign with the bulk of his best troops, this is the same time frame we can finally trace the total abandonment of the Romans from Britain. The year 383 AD, when this Emperor departs Britain, is the last date for any evidence of the Roman *military* presence in Wales, the western Pennines, and the historical region of Deva (the non-Romanized part of Britain, south of Hadrian's Wall). Several near-contemporary or early medieval accounts of this era tell us more about the Roman departure from Britain. The early medieval historian, Gildas, tells us in his work *De Excidio et Conquestu Britanniae*, which he penned down around 540 AD, that Magnus Maximus left Britain never to return, taking with him his troops, governors, auxiliaries, and so on. His practical course was thus to leave the province's authority in the hands of local rulers. In this regard, he could be seen as the restorer of Briton rule across the region. Thus, we can see in the legendary Welsh tales that there are striking comparisons with the historical facts. Soon after departing Britain and becoming Emperor of the Western Roman Empire, Magnus Maximus returned to Britain. He undertook a campaign against the invading Irish Gaels, the Scots, and the native Picts. This was likely done in support of native tribes and allies of Rome: the Votadini, Novantae, and Damnonii. He probably arranged for a formal transfer of authority to the local native chieftains during this time. It is due to this reason that both the Welsh and Galloway kings would claim descent from Magnus Maximus. Alas, the latter was killed in 388 AD, and Britain was finally out of Roman hands. A series of regional governors ruled in the south of Britain until 407 AD, but there is no evidence that they attempted to regain lost territories. Thus, 383 AD is considered the absolute end of the Roman era in Wales.

After the Roman era ended in the region, a new page in Welsh history was opened. Many opportunities now arose for the resurgence and formation of a distinct Welsh identity and a new flow of its history. Some historians have unjustly described this post-Roman era as the

Dark Age of Wales, which is incorrect. It was not a Dark Age figuratively but rather metaphorically. This is mainly because history lacks much material on the post-Roman era. Indeed, it remains a very obscure and complicated period of classic Welsh history, but still, we know enough to paint a definitive picture of an evolving and recovering Wales.

It is important to note that after the departure of Roman troops, Wales was left vulnerable for the most part. This left it open to new invaders and settlers. The foremost of these were tribes from neighboring Ireland. They crossed the waters in considerable numbers, belonging to the groups of Laigin, Uí Liatháin, and the Déisi. History does not know the exact nature of their arrival in Wales. Many theories exist, dubbing them invaders, raiders, migrants, or simple settlers. There is a possibility that Wales suffered from a plague and was depopulated in some parts, which made way for the arrival of the Irish. Either way, the Irish settled when the Romans were gone. However, they did not sweep over the whole of Wales but concentrated more on the southern and western coasts and in Cornwall. They were also present in Anglesey and Gwynedd. In search of new lands to populate, the Irish brought their characteristic round huts and monumental inscription stones. Of the latter, many are found across the coastal regions of Wales and feature inscriptions in Latin and Ogham, the classic Irish script involving a series of lines. As a result of this small-scale Irish settlement in Wales, it can be safely assumed that the modern Welsh nation does contain a small portion of Irish genealogy or at least cultural influence. The Medieval Welsh Royal genealogies include some Irish-named ancestors, who also appear in the native Irish story "The Expulsion of the Déisi."

Particular light must be shed on the misrepresented post-Roman era of Wales, which is unjustly described as a dark age of war and squalor. It was undoubtedly a period of significant political and religious change, cultural development, and major social evolution.

According to the historian Geraint H. Jenkins, four distinct aspects define the post-Roman period: the emergence of multiple political kingdoms, the codification of the native laws, the vital missions of the Welsh saints, the genesis of the Welsh language and the vernacular literature. All these aspects combined helped to shape the future of the Welsh nation and to introduce Wales as a recognizable territorial and cultural entity. However, it was not a unified state but a group of self-governing kingdoms.

When the Romans withdrew, the many small British (Welsh) states and petty kingdoms were left to govern themselves. There was only some sporadic Roman influence left, mainly in aspects of governance and political terms. For example, one inscribed stone from Gwynedd, dated to the late 5th and early 6th centuries, commemorates a certain Cantiorix, a man described as *cives* (citizen) of Gwynedd and a cousin of Magos the *magistratus* (magistrate). These titles are of Roman and Latin origin.

Christianity was Wales's most important new facet after the Romans were gone. This new religion, no longer persecuted since the mid-300s AD, was quick to spread in Early Medieval British Isles and Ireland. It was also quick to take root in Wales, which was thoroughly Christian in this period. The nature of Christianity in the whole of Britain (Wales included) was centered on monasticism. However, the origins of the religion in this region are somewhat obscure. The Church was "episcopally-dominated" and consisted of many monasteries. Of course, as is common with this religion, the monasteries and religious communities were mainly situated around good, fertile land, most of which belonged to the church.

Archeology played a massive part in understanding the nature of Christianity in post-Roman Wales. We know now that these Christian Britons, once the Romans were gone, continued their practice of extended cyst burials, an ancient heathen tradition that was changed into a Christian character—judging from the locations of these burials, which are found in the southernmost Scottish Lowlands, Wales, and the west country of England, the lands of the native Britons. Cyst burials involve long slabs of stones that line a grave. The deceased is placed relatively frugally, with no grave goods, oriented east to west. This funerary practice is the earliest form of Christian burial; in later eras, the cemeteries were almost always placed beside a church or a monastery. Most notably, these burials allow us to distinguish clearly from Anglo-Saxon burials, which are different. Either way, the churches and monasteries served to play an essential part in the development of post-Roman Wales. The income for the church was landed proprietorship, agriculture, animal husbandry (raising of sheep, pigs, and goats), infrastructure (threshing floors and barns), and the employment of stewards for labor supervision.

Furthermore, lands under clerical proprietorship were exempt from the fiscal demands of kings and lords. The church was a place of peace; it had the power of *nawdd* (protection) and was considered a *noddfa* (a sanctuary). Overall, the Church was more than simply a spiritual institution; it served a purpose in the infrastructure and development of Wales. The Church was prominent in early medieval Wales. So much so that the period from 500 to 700 AD is often called the "Age of Saints." This period is marked by the busy creation of monastic settlements throughout the country and the rise of religious leaders and saints, such as Saint Teilo, Saint David, and Saint Illtud. Saint David, for example, is one of Wales's early Welsh saints and also its patron saint. Catholic Encyclopedia gives us a good summary of his life and role in early medieval Wales:

"Bishop and Confessor, patron of Wales. He is usually represented standing on a little hill with a dove on his shoulder. From time immemorial, the Welsh have worn a leek on St. David's day, in memory of a battle against the Saxons, at which it is said they wore leeks in their hats, by St. David's advice, to distinguish them from their enemies. He is commemorated on 1 March. The earliest mention of St. David is found in

a tenth-century manuscript Of the "Annales Cambriae," which assigns his death to A.D. 601. Many other writers, from Geoffrey of Monmouth down to Father Richard Stanton, hold that he died about 544, but their opinion is based solely on data given in various late "lives" of St. David, and there seems no good reason for setting aside the definite statement of the "Annales Cambriae," which is now generally accepted. Little else that can claim to be historical is known about St. David. The tradition that he was born at Henfynyw (Vetus-Menevia) in Cardiganshire is not improbable. He was prominent at the Synod of Brevi (Llanddewi Brefi in Cardiganshire), which has been identified with the important Roman military station, Loventium. Shortly afterward, in 569, he presided over another synod held at a place called Lucus Victoriae. He was Bishop (probably not Archbishop) of Menevia, the Roman port of Menapia in Pembrokeshire, later known as St. David's, then the chief point of departure for Ireland. St. David was canonized by Pope Callistus II in the year 1120."

Chapter IV

Early on, Wales consisted of many small kingdoms after the Romans were gone. The origins, emergence, and extent of these kingdoms are still relatively obscure in history, and there is still a lot to be learned. Of course, a lot is left to speculation. By the 6th century AD, numerous minor kings existed, some of which held areas as small as 24 km (15 mi) in radius. Such petty kingdoms most likely existed near the coast. However, over time, certain kingdoms rose above the others, and many simply disappeared into the larger ones. A period of dynastic strengthening existed in certain areas, which led to the disappearance of weaker, smaller petty kingdoms and the rise of more powerful ones. Still, there is a significant absence of information about many of these kingdoms, and all we know for sure pertains to the larger ones that lived on for centuries. For example, there is better documentation relating to the realms of the southeast, which shows us a long and slow property acquisition famed Meurig ap Tewdrig, the son of Saint Tewdric. He was the King of the early medieval Welsh kingdoms of Gwent and Glywysing. He likely lived sometime around 596 to 665 AD. His father abdicated from the throne of Gwent in his son's favor and retreated to the Tintern Abbey to live a hermit's life. It is undoubtedly worth mentioning, even briefly, the historical figure of Meurig, as it can be a valuable insight into the early medieval history of Wales. Meurig ap Tewdrig took over Gwent after his father and later managed to reunite it with the minor kingdom of Ergyng (which the English later called Archenfield). This he did by marrying Onbrawst, the daughter of Ergyng King Gwrgan Fawr (Gwrgan the Great). Meurig was the father of Athrwys ap Meurig, a historical figure linked with the enigmatic hero of legend, King Arthur, the ruler who drove out the invading Saxons. It is believed that Athrwys died before his father Meurig, and his grandson, Morgan Mwynfawr, thus succeeded the latter.

These figures are essential in the context of a new struggle in Welsh history, the fight against the Anglo-Saxons. These early Welsh kings fought the invading Germanic tribes that were already sweeping across the south of Britain and establishing their independent kingdoms there. Meurig rose to defend his realm but found the struggle too great. Because of this, he asked his father for help: and even though a hermit in a monastery, Tewdrig answered his son's call and ventured into battle one more time. Together, father and son decisively defeated an invading Saxon army in the Battle of Pont y Saeson (Bridge of the Saxons), sometime around 630 AD. They won a great victory, but Tewdrig was mortally wounded. He asked to be buried on the small holy isle of Flat Holm in the Bristol Channel, but he never managed to get there. He died en route, and his son buried him near the Severn estuary, *Mateyrn*, "the Place of the King." A great church was built at the burial spot. Today, the place is called Mathern.

The Battle of the Bridge of the Saxons was not the first such clash with the new invading enemies. Britain did not get a solid chance to regain its independence after the Romans departed. A wave of new Germanic tribes descended across the North Sea and devastated its shores. The Jutes, the Angles, and the Saxons were fierce seafaring warriors that dwelt on the shores of modern Denmark and North Germany. Seeking new lands to colonize, they found the British Isles ripe for plucking. From roughly 420 AD, they began settling the eastern British coasts in a series of migrations. The exact nature of their arrival is based on scant historical information. Likely, they were initially invited to settle in these coastal regions in exchange for their military assistance. At the time, the Romano-British rulers had great difficulties dealing with the invading armies of Picts and Scots. Since the Germanic Angles and Saxons were well known for their military prowess, they were invited over to help. However, this situation gradually evolved into large-scale settlements and conflicts, thus a new era in the history of Britain.

Sadly, the arrival of the Anglo-Saxons marked the beginning of the end for the native Britons of modern England. However, Wales largely avoided such a fate. This is a very active period for post-Roman and Early Medieval Britain. Boundaries changed very often as productive and attractive land was in high demand. Undoubtedly, it was a very turbulent and violent period in the region's history; the period termed the "Dark Age of Britain." This can be quickly deduced when you consider that not only the Brythonic petty kingdoms warred amongst themselves, but there were also the invading Angles and Saxons, as well as Irish, Pictish, and Scot raiders. All these ethnicities and troops combined warranted a challenging period for Wales and the whole of the Brythonic realm. Very early on, the Anglo-Saxons established their small kingdoms in the south of Britain. From there began a series of expansions that would last centuries and, in the end, overwhelm and extinguish the native Brythonic identity of what is today England.

But what of Wales? In that regard, the most important aspects are the expansions of the Anglo-Saxon petty Kingdoms of Mercia, Wessex, and Northumbria. Even around this early time, the natural boundary between Wales and England began forming as a significant, 180-mile-long defensive boundary. Of course, this boundary would see the most action since it was the only thing that kept the Anglo-Saxons at bay. The Welsh kingdoms situated there were in the direct path of the raiders and invaders: these were the Kingdoms of Gwynedd, Powys, and Gwent. These, and other Welsh kingdoms, stood proudly and bravely in the face of the new invaders, ready to sacrifice everything to preserve their culture, traditions, and Brythonic identity. They continued to defend their lands even after their fellow countrymen, notably those in the north in the Yr Hen Gogledd (The Old North) and the east, had fallen under the Saxons. By fighting fiercely and preserving their last remaining boundary, the Welsh maintained their identity and paved the way for the untroubled formation of Wales as we know it today.

In the face of overwhelming danger, the Welsh sought unity and stuck to their identity. It was around this time that the term Y Cymru (the name for Wales) and Cymru (for its inhabitants) emerged, roughly translated to "Fellow Countrymen." It was a clear distinction against the newcomers, the Anglo-Saxons. The term was an apparent attempt to emphasize that the Welsh and the Men of the North were the same people, with a single language and shared history. However, with the interference of the Anglo-Saxons, these peoples became increasingly separated, and the remaining Welsh kingdoms soon became a place of sanctuary and refuge for the defeated Brythonic leaders from across Britain, especially from the north. The north was embroiled in a bitter conflict with the Anglo-Saxon kingdoms of Bernicia and Deira. From their arrival in the mid-400s AD, the Anglo-Saxons would carve their way through Britain and make many attempts at Wales across several centuries. However, there is always the bigger "fish in the *North* Sea." The fearsome Vikings burst onto the world's stage in 793 AD after raiding the Anglo-Saxon monastery at Lindisfarne. This ushered in the Viking Age and plunged the British Isles into a new epoch of struggle and war.

However, for now, let us reflect upon the Anglo-Saxon age. From the beginning, the Welsh, and the Britons in general, gave the invaders their fiercest resistance. A series of battles, some shrouded in myth and legend, are documented. Of course, the famed Battle of Badon Hill is one of the most important battles against the invaders. Sadly, not much is known for sure about this clash. Scholars have studied it for decades, but the information remains scarce. It is likely that the battle occurred sometime around 500 AD and involved a major Brythonic force that the legendary King Arthur led. However, the real identity of this King remains one of the most significant historic enigmas of our time. Either way, the Britons landed a major victory against the invading Anglo-Saxons, stopping their progress for many years. The battle undoubtedly relates to Wales's history as it may have involved some of the Welsh Kingdoms. Sadly, we do not know the exact location of the battle, but many sites are proposed, all near the borders of Wales. The leaders of the Anglo-Saxons are also unknown, but individuals such as Aelle of Bernicia and Cerdic of Wessex (fighting jointly) are proposed. While nothing can be said with certainty about the historicity of such a battle, there is no reason to doubt that it did occur in the late 400s AD, as one of the first major stops on the road of the Anglo-Saxons. Sadly, history leaves us wanting here. The true tales of the enigmatic Brythonic King Arthur are lost to time, and we are left with epic poems and snippets of clues as to his true identity.

In the mythology of Wales and Cornwall, the remnants of the ancient Britons, King Arthur holds a great and special place. In Welsh, he is known as *Brenin Arthur* and in Cornish as *Arthur Gernow*. He was the ruler of Britons who led them to a great victory against the invading Saxons and established a long period of peace for Wales and Cornwall at least. It is unknown who he was in history. Some have proposed that he was the son of Meurig ap Tewdrig, the King of Gwent. Arthur's legendary resting place on the Isle of Avalon remains a great historical mystery. Scholars are still trying to find an actual area within Britain to identify with it. It has been proposed that Avalon is the modern-day hill of Glastonbury Tor, which in ancient times was an island surrounded by marshes. We can read in medieval chronicles that around 1120 AD, monks of the nearby Glastonbury Abbey claimed to have discovered, at a depth of five meters, a wooden tree trunk coffin with the bones of King Arthur and his wife, Guinevere. This they deduced since a lead cross was also found there, bearing the inscription:

Hic jacet sepultus inclitus rex Arturius in insula Avalonia.
("Here lies entombed the renowned king Arthur in the island of Avalon.")

Unfortunately, we do not possess any more factual information about King Arthur as an actual, historic King from Wales or Cornwall. His legend remains a great inspiration for the Brythonic peoples of these two nations. Either way, Arthur's great victory at Badon Hill (around 496 AD) stopped the Saxons but not forever. After a period of stability and peace that Arthur introduced, which lasted about 50 years, the Anglo-Saxons resumed their advance. After 550 AD, war once again continued across Britain. The forces of the Angles and the Saxons, from their respective kingdoms, are focused on the Welsh and Cornish to the south and the Britons of the Old North. Many battles were fought, and the invaders began decimating the Britons gradually. In 577 AD, for example, the Battle of Deorham, near Bath, was fought. It was recorded in the Anglo-Saxon Chronicle that the Kingdom of Wessex defeated the Brythonic Kingdoms of Devon and Cornwall. Their victory captured the strategically important towns of Gloucester, Bath, and Cirencester, all wealthy and relatively sophisticated. Their loss was a heavy blow for the Britons. Of course, with their gradual victories, the Anglo-Saxons managed to divide the Britons more and more in geographic terms. The Briton defeat at Deorham meant that the land contact between the Kingdoms of Wales and those in Devon and Cornwall was now lost. They were cut off from one another. This began the gradual differentiation of Wales and Cornwall, which made their languages essentially different.

A similar and even more critical event happened in 616 AD (possibly even earlier, in 605 AD). This year, the Battle of Chester was fought between the Anglo-Saxon Kingdom of Northumbria, led by King Æthelfrith, and the Welsh armies from Gwynedd and Powys. It was a significant defeat for the Welsh. Their leaders, King Selyf ap Cynan and Cadwal Crysban, were slain, along with many Christian monks who came to pray for their cause. Historical accounts, notably the Anglo-Saxon Chronicle, mention the battle:

"And here Æðelfrið led his army to Chester, and there slew countless Welsh. And came about Augustinus's prophecy, that he said, "If they do not have peace with us, they will die at the hands of the Saxons." There also were slain 200 priests who came there to pray for the Welsh army. Scrocmail was called their leader, and he escaped as one of fifty."

This defeat resulted in the significant loss of life and Briton nobility and the severing of the land connection between the Kingdoms of Wales and their countrymen in the Old North (Brythonic Kingdoms of Rheged and Strathclyde). Following this severing, the fate of the Old North was sealed. Its inhabitants were essentially Welsh. They spoke Cumbric, a dialect of the Old Welsh language, and they were considered one people, but when their land connection was severed, they were left to their fates. All the small kingdoms of the Old North, except Strathclyde, were conquered by the Picts and the Anglo-Saxons by 800 AD. Strathclyde held out but was later incorporated into the rising Middle-Irish-speaking Kingdom of Scotland. In the 12th century AD, the Cumbric language and its Brythonic identity were lost. However, the memory of this realm has been preserved in Wales until now.

Chapter V

Onwards, we go with the fate of medieval Wales. From the 8th century AD forward, Wales remained the largest, by far, of the remaining Brythonic areas in Britain. The two others were Cornwall to the south and the kingdoms of Hen Ogledd (the Old North) to the North. Of course, as we said, Wales at this time was divided into many smaller, separate kingdoms. The largest was Powys in eastern Wales and Gwynedd to the Northwest. The latter was the most powerful and became prominent in the 6th and 7th centuries, especially under the rule of Kings Maelgwn Gwynedd, who died around 547 AD, and Cadwallon ap Cadfan, who died around 634 or 635 AD. The latter made a bold move by allying his kingdom with the Anglo-Saxon Kingdom of Mercia, then ruled by its famed King Penda. This alliance allowed them to wage war against another Anglo-Saxon kingdom, Northumbria. In 33 AD, at the Battle of Hatfield Chase near Doncaster, the Welsh King defeated the local ruler, Edwin, and gained control of Northumbria for around a year after sacking the city of York. The early medieval chronicles tell us that Cadwallon bore bitter hatred against the Anglo-Saxons and that he showed them no mercy. Many Northumbrians were massacred as a result. Bede, in his *Ecclesiastical History of the English People*, writes:

"He neither spared the female sex, nor the innocent age of children, but with savage cruelty put them to tormenting deaths, ravaging all their country for a long time, and resolving to cut off all the race of the English within the borders of Britain."

Alas, Cadwallon ap Cadfan was slain in battle not long after, in 634 AD, fighting against Oswald of Northumbria in the Battle of Heavenfield near Hexham, Yorkshire. His successor, Cadafael ap Cynefeddw, pursued a similar policy, allying himself with the mighty King Penda of Mercia. However, he chose not to go on the offensive but rather stay on the defensive, protecting the boundaries of

Gwynedd, and the other realms of Wales, especially in the face of the ever-growing power of the Kingdom of Mercia. In 642 AD, in the Battle of Maserfield in Oswestry, the Mercian King Penda allied himself with prominent Welsh rulers: Kings Cadafael Cadomedd ap Cynefeddw of Gwynedd, Eluan of Powys, and Cynddylan of Pengwern. Together they engaged the hated Oswald of Northumbria and decisively defeated him. The Anglo-Saxon Chronicle speaks of the hatred that Penda of Mercia bore for his enemy, even though he was an Anglo-Saxon. After the defeat, he took Oswald's dead body and dismembered it into pieces, placing each one on a stake.

In general, much of the Welsh (and Brythonic) history after the arrival of the Anglo-Saxons is centered on constant warfare. Granted, this warfare was led, for the most part, outside the boundaries of the Welsh Kingdoms. Each century was marked by numerous battles, shifts in power, ups and downs of kingdoms, and a constant change of kings and boundaries. The Anglo-Saxon Kingdoms also warred between themselves, and in the early 800s, there was an increased and bitter conflict between Mercia and Wessex. In 821 AD, this conflict culminated at the Battle at Basingwerk, near Hollywell in Flintshire. Here, the Mercian King Coenwulf was slain in battle. This Mercian defeat brought a tremendous shift in power, as Wessex now had the dominant role, and the Mercian power began to wane. In 825 AD, another battle was fought between these two Kingdoms, the Battle of Ellendun, in Wiltshire. It involved Kings Ecgberht of Wessex and Beornwulf of Mercia. The battle was another Wessex victory, effectively ending Mercian supremacy in the South of England. Undoubtedly, this change in power did affect the Welsh kingdoms.

Let us stop here for a moment and reflect upon the fearsomeness of the early medieval Welsh. Their resilience, willingness to preserve their identity, and undeniable struggle to repulse the foreign, Anglo-Saxon invaders cannot be overlooked. The ferocity of the Welsh people, the prowess of their Brythonic warriors, and the undying hope for their future helped them retain their identity from before the Roman times until today. Of course, the success of their defensive struggle had many roots in Wales's favorable geographic position. Invading it successfully was a great challenge; a linear natural border was easy to defend. Of all these Kingdoms, besides Gwynedd, Powys rose as a prominent entity. It was the easternmost of the major realms and came under tremendous pressure from the Anglo-Saxons in Cheshire, Shropshire, and Herefordshire. Originally, Powys extended eastward into the areas today located in England. Likewise, its ancient capital, Pengwern, has today been identified with modern Shrewsbury, or perhaps a site north of Baschurch. These areas were ultimately lost to the Mercians as Powys was at the forefront of the attacks.

One of the more unique medieval constructions was built in this area, the so-called "Offa's Dyke". It is a tremendous earthen barrier, a linear earthwork that roughly follows the boundary between Wales and England. The creation of this dyke, just as the name suggests, has been attributed to a prominent King of Mercia, Offa. He was frequently at war with the many Welsh kingdoms, as is recorded by the near-contemporary accounts such as the _Annales Cambriae_. In AD 760, he fought the Welsh at Hereford and conducted further campaigns in Wales in 778, 784, and 796 AD. Undoubtedly the best association with this Mercian King is Offa's Dyke, which is attributed to him and likely constructed by his command. Whether it was completed within his lifetime is not known. The great earthwork could have marked an agreed border between Wales and Mercia.

Furthermore, such linear earthworks are not unknown in ancient history and can be found across Europe. One of the earliest mentions that links Offa with this dyke was written by the medieval monk Asser in his biography of King Alfred the Great. He writes, "a certain vigorous King, called Offa, had a great dyke built between Wales and Mercia from sea to sea." After all, everything points to the fact that Offa ordered its construction. Modern historiography has no reason to doubt this, even though the exact date of the building has not been affirmed by archeological testing. The earliest recorded name for the dyke, both in Welsh and English, mentions Offa, confirming this. However, from what we can see today, the dyke likely did not stretch from sea to sea but instead covered some two-thirds of the length of the border, possibly due to the lay of the land. In the north, the dyke ends near Llanfynydd, some 5 miles (8 km) from the coast, and in the south, it stops at Rushock Hill, a site near Kington in Herefordshire less than 50 miles (80 km) from the Bristol Channel.

Offa's Dyke is not the only such earthwork at the Welsh borders. Also extant is Wat's Dyke, amongst others, less preserved. It is not known which one was built first. Still, they both provide us with crucial information: the Anglo-Saxons perhaps realized that the Welsh Kingdoms were a goal too hard to handle, so they sought to establish a defensive border to separate themselves for good. Indeed, it was also a strategic Mercian build: it offered commanding views into Wales and was likely erected in the place the Mercians chose as best. From what can be observed, Offa's Dyke was an immense task for the era. It required an extensive workforce and an incredible amount of money. This shows that the Mercian King did not spare his expenses regarding keeping the Welsh at bay. That's how big of a threat these fierce Britons were.

Either way, what Wales needed in the Middle Ages was unity. Having a semblance of a state divided into several smaller kingdoms would never work for the benefit of the Welsh as a whole. However, by the 9th century, certain domains rose in power, and rulers came about that would govern a vast majority of the Welsh. The first king that would rule a big part of Wales was one Rhodri ap Merfyn, also known as Rhodri Mawr, or Rhodri the Great, who was originally a King of Gwynedd. He came to the throne of that kingdom in 844 AD and went on to annex Powys in 856 and Seisyllwg in 871 AD. With these acquisitions, his realm encompassed much of modern Welsh territory.

However, upon his death, his six sons divided the lands amongst themselves, but it was Rhodri's grandson, Hywel Dda (Hywel the Good), who managed to form the kingdom of Deheubarth. He did this by joining the smaller domains of the southwest together, extending his rule across most of Wales by 942 AD. Hywel Dda is commonly associated with codifying the extant Welsh law at a council he assembled at Whitland. From then on, the rules were called "Laws of Hywel."

Interestingly and cunningly, Hywel pursued a peace policy with the English kingdoms. Alas, he died in 949 AD leaving his sons in control of Deheubarth. However, they soon lost Gwynedd in a power struggle with that realm's original ruling dynasty. Now, Wales faced a new crisis: the Vikings. These fearsome northern seafarers had already established themselves across the British and Scottish Isles: in the Shetlands, Orkneys, Ireland, Isle of Man, Hebrides, Faroe Islands, and England. Wales suffered Danish raids between 950 and 1000 AD, particularly at Anglesey. From here, according to the medieval chronicle Brut y Tywysogion, one particular Viking, named Godfrey Haroldson, carried off two thousand captives in 987 AD. The King of Gwynedd at the time, Maredudd ab Owain, had to pay him a considerable ransom to get his kinsmen back from slavery. In the end, it wasn't until the early 1000s that Wales was united under one ruler. This man was Gruffydd ap Llywelyn, the only man to join Wales under his kingship. He started as a King of Gwynedd, but by 1057 AD, he was the ruler of Wales as a whole and even annexed small parts of England beyond the borders. What is more interesting is that he continued his reign without internal strife or battles. Alas, his kingship over a united Wales was not to last. Historian John Davies sums it up thus:

"[Gruffydd ap Llywelyn] was the only Welsh king ever to rule over the entire territory of Wales... Thus, from about 1057 until his death in 1063, the whole of Wales recognized the kingship of Gruffydd ap

Llywelyn. For about seven brief years, Wales was one, under one ruler, a feat with neither precedent nor successor."

The reign of Gruffydd ap Llywelyn is undoubtedly significant for our story of the history of Wales. The period in which he reigned is indeed a turning point, with the history of the British Isles on the brink of an entirely new era, an era beyond the Vikings, the Anglo-Saxons, and the wars of the early Middle Ages. As we said, Gruffydd began as the King of Gwynedd and gradually expanded his realms across Wales. In 1055 AD, he killed his chief rival, Gruffydd ap Rhydderch, in battle and recaptured the kingdom of Deheubarth. His reign helped Wales enter a period of relative peace and stability until at least 1063 AD.

After expanding his reign, Gruffydd allied himself with Ælfgar, son of Leofric, Earl of Mercia. By that time, the Anglo-Saxon realms were united under the Kingdom of the English from the time of Alfred the Great. Now, the Earl of Mercia lost his earldom in East Anglia to the King of the English, Harold Godwinson, and his brothers. Now he allied himself with the Welsh King, and together they set out on Hereford. There, they were opposed by the Earl of Hereford, Ralph the Timid, whom they bested and set Hereford on fire. The city was sacked, and the wooden motte-and-bailey castle was set aflame. Subsequently, Ælfgar was restored to his Earldom, and with the help of Gruffydd, he concluded a peace treaty.

Ultimately, with his territories expanded, Gruffydd was recognized as the King of Wales, a title also recognized by the English. Alas, his bountiful reign was not to last long. Gruffydd was vulnerable when his chief ally, Ælfgar, died in 1062 AD. That same year, the English magnate, Harold Godwinson, was approved to launch a surprise attack on the Welsh at their court at Rhuddlan. In this attack, Gruffydd barely avoided captivity and escaped to sea in his last ship in the nick of time. In early 1063, Tostig Godwinson, Harold's brother, led an army into northern Wales in unison with his brother's army attacking from the south. Gruffydd, on the run, tried to find refuge in the wild hills of Snowdonia, where ultimately, he met his end. His enemies, who likely bore him great hatred, beheaded his corpse and sent his head, as well as the figurehead of his ship, to Harold Godwinson. Who exactly killed Gruffydd is not known. The medieval Ulster Chronicle writes that it was Cynan ap Iago, whose father had been previously put to death by Gruffydd in 1039. Either way, Gruffydd did not lack enemies, which he gained in his expansion. Harold went on to marry Gruffydd's widow, although their marriage would last only three years until his death. Most importantly, Wales did not remain unified as a single realm but was again divided into the traditional kingdoms. The two sons of Gruffydd later attempted to regain parts of their father's lost empire but were defeated in the Battle of Mechain in 1069.

Did You Know?

Tafolwern Castle is an excellent insight into the tumultuous Welsh Middle Ages. It was built between the Afon Twymyn and the Afon Rhiw Saeson in Powys, likely by the noble Owain Cyfeiliog, who was given the commote of Cyfeiliog by his uncle, Madog ap Maredudd. In 1160 AD, the castle was taken by the famed Owain Gwynedd, but just two years after, in 1162, it was taken by Hywel ap Ieuaf, Lord of Arwystli. Owain Gwynedd defeated Hywel in the Battle of Llanidloes, rebuilt the castle, and returned it in 1165 to Owain Cyfeiliog. Alas, the latter sided with the Normans, and the castle was soon taken from him (again) by the powerful Rhys ap Gruffydd. The Normans then came to the aid of Cyfeiliog and helped him retake the castle. This is just a snippet of this castle's terrible fate. There are similar stories across Wales, which has a far greater density of castles than any other nation in the world. This proves how difficult it was to conquer Wales and how the Welsh were keen on fighting all invaders.

In the meantime, one cardinal event struck England and the whole British Isles, the 1066 Norman Invasion. Following the death of the English King, Edward the Confessor, this year, many claimants rushed to claim the vacant throne. The succession crisis left England vulnerable, and Edward's hastily elected heir, Harold Godwinson, soon faced adversaries from every side. To the north, it was the Norwegian King, Harald Hardrada, pressing his claims. Godwinson hastily marched his armies from south to north and managed to crush the Norwegian army at the Battle of Stamford bridge. However, almost simultaneously, a much bigger foe landed on the southernmost shores of England: William the Bastard, the fearsome Norman Duke of Normandy. With a vast army, he sailed across the English channel, boasting his rightful claim to the throne of England. At the time, the Normans were amongst the best warriors in Europe and had introduced several innovations into medieval society. With no more options at his disposal, Harold Godwinson rushed his exhausted army in a forced march down south, where he was defeated and killed in the fateful Battle of Hastings in 1066 AD.

This ushered in a new age for England and its neighbors: the Norman Age. From 1066 onwards, William the Conqueror, as he was now called, stabilized his rule over the British Isles and introduced Norman feudalism, castle building, and other essential changes. To no one's surprise, as soon as they swept across England, the Normans also set their sights on Wales. In the early days, between 1067 and 1081 AD, the pressure on Wales was not so great since William the Conqueror had to stabilize his grasp over England first. However, after 1081 AD, the pressure significantly increased. It didn't take long for the entirety of Wales to be under the control of William's son, William II, who controlled it by 1094. This was made all the easier by the power vacuum left in Wales after the death of Gruffydd ap Llewelyn. Without his unifying presence, the regional kings of Wales squabbled amongst themselves, staying vulnerable to Norman attacks.

As before, the Welsh proved challenging to control, and they fervently refused the oppressive chains of foreign invaders. So, they kept up the fight. Every Welsh citizen disliked the Normans and their practices. It wasn't long after that the Welsh collectively struck back at the Normans and began a long fight to regain their independence. By 1101 AD, they had regained control of most of their nation, especially under the long reign of the famed King Gruffudd ap Cynan, whose exceptionally long life and reign were marked by many shining achievements. Most notably, he escaped the Norman captivity after 12 years and struck back at his oppressors. He also gained some assistance from King Magnus III Barefoot of Norway, who launched a brief attack on the Normans close to the Isle of Anglesey, near Baffin Island (Ynys Seiriol). After that, he killed the Norman Lord, Hugh of Montgomery, 2nd Earl of Shrewsbury. Even after Gruffudd, the struggle continued and exhausted both sides. Under the rule of the fourth son of William, King Henry I, the Normans pushed westwards into Wales, being now well consolidated in England. However, it was soon apparent that both sides wanted peace more than to continue to struggle and more battles. This resulted in a sort of standoff that lasted from 1135 to 1154.

Chapter VI

At this point, it is essential to mention that the encroachment of the Normans was not aggressive. Every large-scale invasion is multi-faceted, and this one was too. The Welsh were affected and influenced by the Normans in numerous ways. Adopting many of the Norman traits and traditions, the Welsh nobles began erecting Norman-style castles and followed the Norman way of creating new towns. With this, trade was promoted, the economy was boosted, and further work opportunities arose across the country. Also, the Norman influence could have been observed in the Church too. The old Celtic Welsh Church had long before conformed to the practices of Latin Christendom. With the arrival of the Normans and their cultural pressure, the Welsh adopted the diocesan organization of the Roman Church. This resulted in the erection of several new and vital cathedrals in the first half of the 12th century. These include St. Asaph in Flint, Bangor in Caernarvon, St. David's in Pembrokeshire, and Llandaff in Cardiff. Numerous Cistercian monasteries followed these. However, with all these changes, it is safe to say that the Welsh identity and traditions were alive and not lost. Throughout this period, the famed epic poems of the Cymry, which were up to that point transmitted only orally, were now written down for the first time. Also penned down in this era was the famed "Historia Regum Britanniae," an epic and mostly fictional history of the ancient Kings of Britain, written by the Norman Geoffrey of Monmouth. He later became the Bishop of St. Asaph. The book was amongst the most famous works in medieval Welsh society and instilled pride in the hearts of the Welsh. The most significant part of this "history" was the legendary romantic story of King Arthur, the famed leader of the Britons. However, the Welsh most importantly retained their national characteristics that gave them their unique identity and distinguished them from the Saxons and Normans. Near the end of the 12th century, the half-Welsh, half-Norman writer Gerald of Wales (known as Giraldus Cambrensis) tells us that the Welsh are light and active, stubborn and quick to take offense, hardy and warlike, but full of family pride, frugal in food, drink, and dress, and even so religious and passionately devoted to poetry and music.

Did You Know?

One of the most ancient Welsh sports is called cnapan. It was documented in the earliest Middle Ages and was even then an old sport. It is commonly associated with modern-day rugby that is played in Wales. The ancient game involved up to 1,500 naked men playing simultaneously. In the later centuries, clothes were worn. The rules for the game were relatively simple and somewhat obscure: there existed two teams, usually from two neighboring villages. The teams played with a small wooden ball soaked in oil to make it slippery and harder to catch. The "goals" were the team's home parish and were up to two miles away, and the ball had to be scored in whatever way possible. It was a brutal game that died out in the 18th century, surpassed by standardized rugby. Cnapan is not the only Welsh game of old. Bando also existed, similar to hockey, and chwarae pel, a handball game. Both enjoyed great popularity across ancient Wales.

By the time of King Henry II of England, the campaigns of the English had been renewed, and a new expedition into Wales began in 1157 AD. What resulted was a devastating and humiliating defeat for the English, as the Welsh once more proved their worth and ferocity. One of the critical defeats was at the Battle of Ewloe at Coleshill, fought in July 1157 AD. Here, Henry II was almost slain in the fighting and barely escaped together with his routed, panicked army. It wasn't until 1163 that he made another attempt. Still, his success was hardly extant. In 1165 AD, he suffered another defeat (inconclusive by some) at the Battle of Crogen in the Ceiriog Valley. Wales was not to be easily subdued and kept proving that. Some later sources relate that Henry now received an "unclear" form of homage from the two leading "princes" of Wales, Owain Gwynedd, and Rhys ap Gruffydd, at the time, the most powerful nobles of Wales. However, this homage was a catalyst for a Welsh revolt and led to Henry's defeat at Crogen. By this point, it was becoming evident that Henry would never subdue Wales entirely and that he would have to seek a compromise with its lead nobles.

However, in 1170, the mighty prince Owain Gwynedd died, throwing his Kingdom of Gwynedd into a bloody struggle for the throne. His heir Hywel dies within weeks, and his illegitimate son Dafydd usurps the Gwynedd throne. Still, he fails to maintain his hold on southern Wales and loses it to Prince Rhys ap Gruffydd. In the very next year, Henry II enters Wales and meets amicably with Rhys ap Gruffydd, now the most powerful of the Welsh nobles. The English King makes an offering at the shrine of St. David and leaves Wales, setting sail from Pembroke to Ireland. In 1172 we learn that Rhys ap Gruffydd is now the justice of south Wales, appointed by Henry II. This meant that he was essentially the ruler while Henry was gone. In 1176, Rhys hosted a gathering of musicians, bards, performers, and nobles to celebrate his powerful new position. This is the first documented *eisteddfod*, a festival with several ranked competitions, including poetry and music.

The next period of Medieval Welsh history is marked by the rise of one of its best and most successful leaders, or kings. It is the time of Llywelyn ab Iorwerth, also known as Llywelyn Fawr (the Great), who arose from the fierce power struggle unfolding in Gwynedd. Eventually, he became one of the most outstanding Welch leaders that Wales ever had. He ousted his competitors and became the sole ruler of Gwynedd in 1200 AD, and by the time he died in 1240 AD, he ruled most of Wales. His court and "base of operations" was situated on the Welsh north coast, at Abergwyngregyn, where he overlooked the Menai strait from a strategic position. Once he became the King of Gwynedd, however, Llywelyn signed a peace treaty with the English King, John.

Moreover, Gwynedd benefited from marrying King John's illegitimate daughter, Joan. This also augmented his power. Soon afterward, in 1208, he claimed the Kingdom of Powys in south Wales for his own after the arrest of his rival Gwenwynwyn ap Owain. This arrest was made on the orders of King John of England in retaliation for Gwenwynwyn's attacks on the English Marcher lords of the South. The relationship between John and Llewelyn was not good either, as the former invaded parts of Gwynedd in 1211 but was repulsed in the following year by Llywelyn. By 1215, the Welsh were mentioned and included in the crucial English law document, the Magna Carta. This was the first document that included both English and Welsh law and a reference to the common acceptance of the lawful judgment of peers. This document mentions, besides other things:

Chapter 56: The return of lands and liberties to Welshmen if those lands and liberties had been taken by English (and vice versa) without a law-abiding judgment of their peers.

Chapter 57: The return of Gruffydd ap Llywelyn, the illegitimate son of Llywelyn ap Iorwerth (Llywelyn the Great), along with other Welsh hostages who were originally taken for "peace" and "good."

Still, the history of the region was changing at a fast pace. King John died in 1218 AD and was succeeded by King Henry III. The new king and prince Llywelyn agreed to the treaty of Worcester; this treaty again confirmed Llywelyn's right to Wales and did so until he died in 1240. He died in his older years in the Cistercian abbey he founded. He dominated Wales for more than 40 years and remains one of the principal rulers of medieval Wales. Historian David Moore writes of him:

"When Llywelyn died in 1240, his principatus of Wales rested on shaky foundations. Although he had dominated Wales, exacted unprecedented submissions, and raised the status of the prince of Gwynedd to new heights, his three major ambitions – a permanent hegemony, its recognition by the king, and its inheritance in its entirety by his heir – remained unfulfilled. His supremacy, like that of Gruffydd ap Llywelyn, had been merely personal in nature, and there was no institutional framework to maintain it either during his lifetime or after his death."

In Llywelyn's place came his son and heir, Dafydd ap Llywelyn. He followed suit as the ruler of Gwynedd but came into conflict with the new English king, Henry III, when the latter did not allow him to inherit his father's position elsewhere in Wales. This grew into a war, which broke out in 1241 AD and then again in 1245 AD. The issue was still at hand when Dafydd ap Llywelyn died suddenly in 1246 at his court at Abergwyngregyn without leaving an heir. Moreover, the other son of the late Llywelyn the Great, Gruffudd ap Llywelyn, died tragically after trying to escape from the Tower of London where he was imprisoned: his makeshift rope broke, and he plummeted to his death in 1244. However, Gruffudd himself had four sons behind him, and upon his death, a period of internal conflict erupted between three of these sons. This internal strife ended in the rise to power of one Llywelyn ap Gruffudd, better known in Welsh history as Llywelyn Ein Llyw Olaf, Llywelyn, Our Last Leader. Through the Treaty of Montgomery, established in 1267 AD, Llywelyn was confirmed in control over a large part of Wales. However, as was almost a routine, conflict loomed dangerously close by. Llywelyn allied himself with Simon de Montfort, an English noble who revolted with many other barons against the English King. This was part of the Second Barons' War of 1264-1267. As a result of Llywelyn's involvement, the English King went to war against him in 1277 AD. Soon after, Llywelyn was simply forced to seek terms, resulting in the Treaty of Aberconwy, significantly restricting his power and authority in Wales.

Again, war broke out when Llywelyn's brother, Dafydd ap Gruffudd, decided to attack Hawarden Castle on Palm Sunday of 1282 AD. Later, on 11th December that same year, Llywelyn was lured into a special meeting in Cilmeri in Builth Wells Castle with some unknown Marcher lords. There, Llywelyn was killed, and his army was devastated. Persevering, his brother Dafydd ap Gruffudd continued his fight against the English, but that fight seemed increasingly hopeless. In the end, it proved thus: Dafydd was captured in June 1283 AD and was hanged, drawn, and quartered at Shrewsbury. It was a torturous death for a gallant Welsh freedom fighter. His death, and that of his brother, effectively ended Welsh independence, and Wales became the first colony of England until it was finally annexed through the Laws in Wales Acts between 1535 and 1542. That is why Llywelyn ap Gruffudd is known in Welsh history as Llywelyn, Our Last Leader.

A brief revolt soon erupted in Wales, led by the distant cousin of Llywelyn ap Gruffudd, one Madog ap Llywelyn. Madog rose in revolt and claimed the "Prince of Wales" title. Although marked by several successes and victories, this revolt soon ran its course and was defeated in just a year. Madog was captured and taken to London, where the thread of his fate was lost. However, it seems that he was imprisoned for life, not executed, and languished in the English dungeons for at least the next decade.

In 1284, the Statute of Rhuddlan was passed, greatly restricting Welsh laws and ending the greater Welsh independence. It provided a constitutional basis for the government of the Principality of Wales from 1284 to 1536. It introduced English common law into Wales but simultaneously allowed the continuance of Welsh legal practices within the principality. From this point on, the English presence within Wales was complete. King Edward I continued the construction of formidable and massive castles across Wales, especially at the boundaries. Thus, he formed a defensive ring of castles that would greatly assist him in dominating Wales. His conquest was crowned by conferring the title "Prince of Wales" to his son and heir in 1301. The title was thus passed down to the heir apparent of the English, or British throne, which is still the tradition to this day. From then on, Wales was effectively a part of England, even though it was entirely different in culture, history, language, and identity.

Did You Know?

The ancient Welsh legends speak of the famous "Thirteen Treasures," which were procured by the wizard Myrddin (Merlin), and all had excellent magical properties. Merlin supposedly took them all and sailed away in his glass boat, never to be seen again. The Welsh believed he was later buried with all his treasures on Enlli Island (Bardsey Island), off the remote tip of Llyn Peninsula. The thirteen treasures are: White-Hilt, the Sword of Rhydderch Hael; The Hamper of Gwyddno Garanhir; The Horn of Brân Galed from the North; The Chariot of Morgan Mwynfawr; The Halter of Clydno Eiddyn; The Knife of Llawfrodedd Farchog; The Cauldron of Dyrnwch, the Giant; The Whetstone of Tudwal Tudglyd; The Coat of Padarn Beisrudd; The Crock and the Dish of Rhygenydd the Cleric; The Chessboard of Gwenddoleu ap Ceidio; The Mantle of Arthur in Cornwall.

The King of England appointed a special Council of Wales, which was sometimes presided over by the heir to the throne. Thus, the Wales that the English conquered was essentially the country that Llywelyn and all his allies ruled. After the 1284 Statute of Rhuddlan, this realm was formed into six new shires. The entire district of Snowdon, which was the last to fall, was made into the three shires of Anglesey,

Merioneth, and Carnarvon. Next, the part of the land that lay between Dee and Conway, and belonged to the King, was now turned into the shire of Flint. Down to the southwest, the lands of Llywelyn's allies, beyond the Dovey, were made into the shires of Carmarthen and Cardigan. Edward I, furthermore, created four new marcher lordships in Wales. These were Chirk (Chirkland), Bromfield and Yale (Powys Fadog), Ruthin (Dyffryn Clwyd), and Denbigh (Lordship of Denbigh); and one in South Wales, Cantref Bychan. He also restored the principality of Powys Wenwynwyn to one Gruffydd ap Gwenwynwyn, the man who had suffered greatly at the hands of Llewelyn. He and his successor Owen de la Pole thus held it as a marcher lordship. Rhys ap Maredudd of Dryslwyn would have been in a similar position in Cantref Mawr, having adhered to the king during Llewelyn's rebellion. Still, he forfeited his lands by rebelling in 1287 AD. A few other minor Welsh nobles submitted in time to retain their lands but became little more than gentry.

Thus, instead of the traditional chiefs in service of the Welsh Prince, the English king's sheriffs and justices now ruled Wales. Nevertheless, much of the old laws remained in place. However, laws in different lordships varied greatly: some preferred to use the old Welsh law, while others preferred the English law. Despite the English conquest, the submitted noble families still thrived and rose to power, and many of the lords ruled in their lordships as kings of old. The great noble families changed from century to century. Around the time of Llywelyn, these were the Clares in Gloucester and Glamorgan, the Bohuns in Brecon, Braoses in Gower, Valence in Pembroke, Lacys in Denbigh, Warenne in Bromfield and Yale, Fitzalan in Oswestry, and Mortimers in Wigmore and Chirk. As you can notice, many of these surnames are Norman in origin. So it was that Llywelyn, justly called "Our Last Leader," was indeed the last prince of independent Wales. From 1284 onwards, the title of the Prince of Wales belonged to the

King of England's eldest son and heir. This tradition has been carried on through the generations to this day.

After a fierce and noble struggle, Wales finally buckled under the English pressure. The ancient Brythonic realm defied them against all odds, for centuries, before finally stepping down. Even so, they did not lose their laws, customs, culture, language, identity, and everything else that made them who they were: the ancient and proud Welsh people. In the late 1880s, William Ewart Gladstone spoke of the Welsh poignantly:

"The Welsh made a very good and a very hard fight against the English in self-defense, and what was the consequence? That the English were obliged to surround your territory with great castles, and the effect of this has been that, as far as I can reckon, more by far than one-half of the great remains of the castles in the whole island south of the Tweed are castles that surround Wales. That shows that Wales was inhabited by men, and by men who valued and were disposed to struggle for their liberties."

Chapter VII

Soon after, the dissatisfaction of the oppressed Welsh patriots began to show. This, of course, was expressed in the form of revolts. The first such uprising occurred in 1316 and was orchestrated by a minor Welsh noble, Llywelyn Bren. The rebellion arose under specific circumstances, mainly due to a significant power vacuum in southern Wales, after the death of Gilbert de Clare in the Battle of Bannockburn in Scotland. With several decisive factors at play and the general dissatisfaction in Wales being great, Llywelyn Bren launched his revolt in 1316 and was quickly joined by many supporters. With roughly 10,000 men at his command, Llywelyn launched a surprise attack on Caerphilly Castle, which he kept besieged for six weeks. Throughout the relatively short-lived revolt, the Welsh attacked several English-garrisoned castles and became quite a threat. The English knew that if such a threat was left unanswered, it could quickly spin out of control. This warranted a massive English response, and the armies soon met in battle. The Welsh were crushed and forced to flee, and Llywelyn soon after gallantly surrendered in exchange for the lives of his men. The revolt ended rather quickly, and Llywelyn was imprisoned in England. However, his gallantry, noble character, and good nature earned him the respect of his English foes, many of whom pleaded with the English King to spare him. Sadly, Llywelyn was executed out of hand, without anyone's orders, by the cruel and sadistic Hugh, the Younger Despenser. His death sent a wave of sadness and hatred for the English across Wales. Even so, the revolt of Llywelyn Bren was the last challenge to English rule until several decades after.

Gradually, Wales and its people had to settle down under the new circumstances of life and accept the ultimate English sovereignty. Many able Welshmen found new opportunities and a life of service in the English armies. This provided an "outlet for the warlike qualities of the Welsh and led to a period of peace in Wales." The Welsh warriors played a unique role in the Medieval English military. They were famed for their revolutionary use of the longbow. The longbow, arguably a Welsh invention, was an unprecedented weapon of the middle ages. It brought such an impressive innovation to the battlefield and was a decisive weapon in many critical battles in European history. The longbow had a massive range that could quickly devastate approaching enemy armies and could not be countered effectively. The Welsh thus played a decisive role in the English victory against the French at the Battle of Crécy in 1346. Even under all these circumstances, the Welsh displeasure at home grew. Life was difficult and oppressed, and the Welsh were not keen to be mastered. In the latter half of the 14th century, decades after the last revolt, this discontent grew immensely. Some notable contributing factors to this discontent were the devastating effects of the Black Death (the Bubonic Plague), which swept through England in 1348 and 1349 AD and left the nation wrapped in misery, death, and poverty. Of course, we cannot overlook the rapacious and overbearing nature of the English lords and officials, especially in such a trying time.

Did You Know?

The Black Death swept Europe with catastrophic results, and Wales was not spared either. It was carried by rat fleas and reached Abergavenny and Carmarthen in Wales in December 1348 AD. Even before this point, the disease was rife across Wales: wet summers and deteriorating climate contributed to rampant disease amongst people and animals. By 1349, at least a quarter of the population of Wales had died from the plague. Because it lacked major and overpopulated towns, Wales suffered less than other areas of Europe. However, the death of the people resulted in a significant lack of monks and lay brothers within monasteries. This, in turn, meant a great scarcity of manuscripts, written records, and chronicles from the second half of the fourteenth century. Lack of rent that resulted from this population drop required heavy taxation on the remaining Welsh people. To escape this taxation, many emigrated to England. Sadly, the plague returned in waves, notably in 1361 and 1369. A poignant account was written in 1349 by one Ieuan Gethin: "We see death coming into our midst like black smoke, a plague which cuts off the young, a rootless phantom with no fair countenance. Woe is me of the shilling in the armpit; it is seething, terrible, wherever it may come, a head that gives pain and causes a loud cry, a burden carried under the arms (bubonic plague resulted in greatly swollen bulbs beneath the armpits), a painful, angry knob, a white lump... the early ornaments of black death, cinders of the peelings of the cockle weed... It is grievous that they should be on fair skin...."

All this eventually culminated in another Welsh revolt, a major one this time that would last some 15 years. It was the rebellion of Owen Glendower (Owain Glyndŵr). Glendower was a Welsh noble educated in London, England, and served under Richard II. He was a descendant of the princely houses of Powys and Deheubarth and greatly influenced the Welsh and their national sentiments. At first, on friendly terms with the English, Owen Glendower soon fell out of favor with them. The troubles began shortly after the deposition of King Richard when one of the more arrogant Marcher lords unlawfully took over lands belonging to Glendower. Adding insult to injury, King Henry IV refused redress when the matter was put forth. This, and further incidents, caused great animosity between Glendower and the English. So much so that he, in the end, chose to revolt. He declared himself the Prince of Wales and began a struggle in 1400 AD, which would last for the following 15 years. It left much of Wales and the border regions devastated as a result. Glendower excelled as a competent commander and guerilla warfare leader and met with specific successes early in the war. He took over Aberystwyth and Harlech castles and soon governed most of Wales. A momentous change came when he made a treaty with the King of France, thus acquiring French support in the war. He also negotiated with the anti-Pope at Avignon for the independence of the Welsh Church from England. He also made alliances at home, in Wales, notably with the Duke of Northumberland and Edmund Mortimer, both leaders of an English revolt against Henry IV. After their victory, the three agreed to divide England and Wales. King Henry did not waste his time and made many military expeditions into Wales to respond to the uprising. However, he was decidedly unsuccessful.

Alas, from 1405 and on, the tables had turned, and the power of Owen Glendower began to wane. He gained little from the support of his allies and began losing his Welsh followers, many of whom chose to accept the free pardon offered by King Henry IV. Another turning point occurred when Glendower penetrated far into England, reaching Worcester, where he was repulsed by Prince Henry. The latter went on to recapture Aberystwyth and Harlech Castles in 1408. Defiant, Glendower continued to offer resistance, leading a guerilla warfare campaign. Alas, defeat seemed inevitable, and Wales was exhausted in every regard. Around 1412, nothing much was heard of Owen Glendower, and by 1415 he had disappeared, and his revolt ended. His final days remain a real mystery for historians, as nothing is known of his death, his possible hideouts, and such. Many theories surround his final resting place, but nothing is known for certain. Wales suffered in the wake of the revolt, with harsh repressive laws being brought. Some historians also criticized Glendower's rebellion as having adverse effects on the country and its citizens. Some contemporary accounts tell of the devastation of the land and might serve as a crucial insight into this dark period.

"Many of the inhabitants of this area have fled with their wives and children to England; the rest are within castles living in terror for their lives. Send help to spare us at once, or the castles and its inhabitants will be destroyed."

Another quote says:

"Owain Glendower's wars... brought such a desolation that green grass grew on the marketplace Llanrwst, called Bryn y Boten... for it was Glendower's policy to bring all things to waste so that the English should find no strength nor resting place in the country."

Welshmen were barred from all aspects of public life. Even so, their morale could not be shaken: the Welsh experienced a great revival of national feeling, pride for their identity and culture, and an unshakable defiant spirit for some new, future freedom. The famed bards of Wales strummed their strings and chords once more, singing songs of old prophecies telling that the Ancient Britons would see the coming of a promised prince who would free them and once more rule in England. One of the greatest Welsh heroes, Owen Glendower, once more awakened all these notions.

Following these events, the following decades brought a whole new era in the history of England and the British Isles. This new era was known as the Wars of the Roses. They would, of course, leave a mark upon Wales as well. In our book on the Wars of the Roses, we wrote to a great extent about these wars and will now only touch upon them superficially and in connection with Wales. The reign of the English King Henry V was marked by some stunning victories against France and plenty of military prowess and gallantry. However, the reign of Henry VI was markedly different and full of disastrous defeats. During both of their reigns, however, the regional lords were becoming more powerful in Wales and England, and the King's hold over them was weakening. These lords were in the Parliament; they appointed the council and could overrule the law courts. More than a hundred lords in the Welsh Marches held "castle and court." Many of these lords waged their private wars, preying upon their weak neighbors and destabilizing the country.

So it was that the powerful and feuding royal families, tracing their genealogies to past kings, began fighting for more power and prestige and separated themselves into two warring parties: the Red Roses and the White Roses. The Reds were the party of Lancastrians, represented by the gallant King Henry VI, while the Whites were the Yorkists. In the prolonged civil war, the War of the Roses, the Yorkists and Lancastrians waged a bitter conflict over the crown, and each side found its supporters. This resulted in the division of Wales: the west of the country supported Lancaster, from Pembroke to Harlech and from Harlech to Anglesey. The east supported York, from Cardiff and Raglan to Wigmore and Chirk. The Lancastrians furthermore held estates in Wales and on the borders. These were the castles of Hereford, Skenfrith, Ogmore, and Kidwelly, all being the regional centers of power and strength. On the other side, the top area of the Yorkists was the march of Wales, centered on Ludlow.

Consequently, the Welsh lords and nobles picked their sides according to their interests and ambitions. Because of this, the Welsh fought against each other at the Battle of Mortimer's Cross, near Wigmore, in February of 1461 AD. In this battle, Owen Tudor died, a prominent Welsh nobleman who married the widow of late King Henry V and thus began a lineage that would later bear the first Tudor monarch of England. This was the fated connection between the thrones of Wales and England. Owen Tudor lost to the young Duke of York, later to be crowned King Edward IV. Owen was taken to Hereford, and his head cut off and placed on the market cross.

Did You Know?

Wales is well known for its excellent production of slate. The Romans used Welsh slate to roof Segontium in Anglesey, and later, King Edward I used it to a great extent to build his many castles to control the Welsh. Slate mines were very active throughout the history of Wales, and during the Industrial Revolution, Welsh slate quarries (owned by the English) were the world's largest slate producers. However, the life of Welsh miners working in these quarries was grim. Slate dust and deplorable working conditions caused rampant tuberculosis and other diseases amongst the poor workers. Long working hours and lack of rights caused further misery. In 1900 the workers of Bethesda Quarry, owned by Lord Penrhyn, finally broke and went on strike, remaining for three years. It was the lengthiest industrial dispute of its time. Wales was always a hotspot for coal, slate mining, and iron works. However, the Welsh who worked there were infamously mistreated. Theirs is a sad fate.

There is no doubt that the Wars of the Roses were brutal and violent in every regard and waged only for the sake of competing royals. The battles were amongst the most violent in British history and spared no one, children, nobles, or commoners. These wars did not pass by the Welsh. The Welsh barons led their men to almost all battles of the Wars of the Roses. Welshmen were often unpredictable allies, and their actions were decisive factors in many a win or loss. Grey of Ruthin, leading the vanguard of the Lancastrian forces in the Battle of Northampton in 1460, deserted to the Yorkist side. His defection caused the battle to be disastrous.

Archers from Wales were infamous for their deadly skills with a long bow. The archers of North Wales, wearing their distinctive three feathers of the Prince of Wales, fought for the Lancastrian side at the great defeat at Towton on Palm Sunday of 1461. The Welshmen of Gwent, talented archers, fought in vain for the Yorkists at the Battle of Edgcote in 1469. After all, the archers were invaluable in these clashes. A notable example is the defiant defense of Harlech Castle, held for the Lancastrians; its stubborn perseverance became the talk of the realm. Either way, all wars have to end. After many years of fighting, with its ups and downs, switching of sides, and many deaths, the Lancastrians and Yorkists fought their last major battle at Tewkesbury in May 1471. Lancaster lost, and the Prince of Wales, the King's only son, perished in the battle. After this, a young Welsh noble, Henry Tudor, the Earl of Richmond (the descendant of that Owen Tudor we mentioned earlier), became the new heir of the Lancastrian cause. Their cause was hopeless, and the young Tudor fled into exile.

It was now the era of the Yorkist Kings, Edward IV, and Richard III; they ruled reasonably well despite all their shortcomings. In Wales, their rule was peaceful and orderly. A Court for Wales was created at Ludlow, and it was from Ludlow that they upheld the law and forced the barons to rule with justice and to obey the king. All indications were that the Yorkists would have a long and uncontested rule, but the regional nobles were not keen on swiftly seeing their power taken away. Jasper Tudor appealed to the Welsh, seeking their loyalty. The men of West Wales, after all, wanted a king who was of their blood and kin ever since the time of Owen Glendower. Tudor made many attempts, in vain, until success finally struck. On August 7th, 1485, the Tudor Earl of Richmond returned from exile and landed at Milford Haven. He was in Wales now and sought allies. He marched on to the valley of the Teifi River, where he was joined by Sir Rees ap Thomas, an influential Welsh noble, together with his army of southern Welshmen. Onwards, he went to the north of Wales, gathering many men to his cause. Even

English nobles joined him as he marched on to Shrewsbury, Tamworth, Lichfield, and Stafford, but the Yorkists were also marching under their King Richard.

The two bitter foes met in battle at Bosworth on August 22nd, 1485, the clash that would be the final battle of the Wars of the Roses. It was a fateful day when the brave King Richard was struck down in the heat of the battle and killed, leading to the final defeat of the Yorkists. Henry Tudor picked up the fallen crown and was crowned king then and there on the battlefield. Thus he became Henry VII, the last Welsh-born King of England and the progenitor of the House of Tudor. He was the grandson of Owen Tudor, a Welsh noble of the Tudors of Penmynydd from the Isle of Anglesey. Henry VII was remembered as a good and competent monarch and was succeeded by his famous son, Henry VIII. Most importantly, the people of Wales welcomed King Henry VII as one of their own, a Welshman who would rule over them justly and righteously.

Did You Know?

The Welsh longbow archers were amongst the most skilled medieval soldiers, and their weapons were devastating in the field. The longbow was developed in Wales, in Gwent, and evolved from the classic short bow. This weapon became popular under the English King Edward I, who recognized its true potential. The English commanders soon discovered that a line of archers, disciplined and trained to hold their line, could easily repulse a charge of armored knights by aiming at the horses. By 1337, Edward III prohibited the practice of all sports except archery and emphasized the manufacture of bows of yew and arrows. In no time, the Welsh longbows became the critical success factor in Medieval battles. A skilled Welshman could fire up to 10 or 15 arrows a minute and had an accurate killing range of over 200 yards. In many medieval battles, especially against the French, these archers would let loose a devastating volley that would quickly demoralize the enemy, decimate their ranks, and send them fleeing.

The Tudors would rule over England and Wales from 1485 until 1603. They were Henry VII, Henry VIII, and their descendants, Edward VI, Mary, and Elizabeth. Under their collective reigns, the people became united, patriotic, prosperous, and law-abiding. Many historians regard the Tudor period as one of the best and most stable in British history. This era prided itself on great poets, adventurers, politicians, and nobles. After all, it is the unwritten rule that after every tumultuous period comes an era of prosperity. Of course, the people of Wales were highly loyal to the Tudors. The royals were dutifully supported by powerful Welshmen such as Sir Rees ap Thomas, the famed Earl of Pembroke, and the diplomatic skills of aristocratic families such as the Cecils. It is important to note that the Tudors were just and efficient rulers but at the same time stern and without mercy. Under them, the law flourished; it could equally defend the weakest classes and crush the highest ones. Welsh were granted some privileges too. Even though their ancient language and culture were regarded as a possible hindrance and source of patriotism, they "obtained the privileges of an equal race, and they were pleased to regard themselves as a dominant one."

"Yours is an ancient language, and the language is connected with an ancient history, and it is connected with an ancient music and with an ancient literature... [Y]our laudable and patriotic efforts will come to be more and more understood and regarded by the English people at large, and that prosperity and honor will attend the meetings by which you endeavor to preserve and to commemorate the ancient history, the ancient

deeds, and the ancient literature of your country, the Principality of Wales."
William Ewart Gladstone, addressing the Welsh.

More importantly, they obtained equal political privileges. The laws were no longer in place that prevented them from residing in garrison towns in Wales or holding land in England. By the Acts of Union of 1535, the whole country, both the shire grounds and march grounds, were divided into one system of shires. They were given representation in the Parliament. As the name suggests, the Acts of Union united Wales and England on equal terms. Of course, since 1284 AD, Merioneth, Flint, Cardigan, Carmarthen, Carnarvon, and Anglesey were all shires, while Glamorgan and Pembroke were governed as such. In 1535, the Welsh marches were also turned into shire ground. Most made up seven new shires: Pembroke, Monmouth, Glamorgan, Montgomery, Denbigh, Brecon, and Radnor. All the others were added to older, pre-existing English and Welsh counties. Alas, those added to Shropshire, Herefordshire, and Gloucestershire became a part of England.

Luckily, Monmouth remained Welsh inseparably, even though it was declared to become an English shire. All this meant that the whole country was governed equally, and Wales was represented in the Parliament, just as England was. Only once was this attempted before, during the reign of Edward II, but without success. Now, it was a reality. Best of all was political equality and the new rule of true law. The Tudors used the Star Chamber, the Court of Wales, and the Great Sessions of Wales to make everyone equal before the law. The Court of Wales was based at Ludlow and was greatly important to the Welsh people. It was represented by some of the most prominent Welshmen, such as the Earl of Pembroke, Sir Henry Sidney, and Bishop Rowland Lee, who struck terror into the entire Welsh Marches between 1534 and 1543. For the peasants, this was a significant and welcome change.

Before, justice had to be sought out at the court of a regional Lord, and justice was not always served for the lowly commoners.

Meanwhile, at the Court of Law at Ludlow, all were equal and had a fair chance. Other than the Court of Wales, which was working for the whole country, a smaller court of justice was held in each of the four groups of shires. These courts were collectively called the Great Sessions of Wales. So it was that although the law was the same for all, Wales still had a separate system. This was mainly because the courts in London were simply too far away from Wales. Shoulder to shoulder with the enhanced justice system and the laws, education also prospered, especially in these regards. Plenty was done to obtain more competent and more educated justices of the peace and fair juries and judges. By the end of the reign of Elizabeth, the last Tudor monarch, it could have been safely said that Wales boasted several privileges and good sides. Notably, these were, according to the historian Sir Owen Morgan Edwards, the following:

"1. There was no hatred between England and Wales; the Welsh gentry served the Queen on land and sea, and the people were more happy and contented than they had been since the time of Llywelyn.

2. There was no danger of private war between lords to which the peasant might be summoned. The brigands which infested parts of the country had been cleared away.

3. The law of land had been fixed. It was determined that land was to go to the eldest son, according to the English fashion. All the land became the property of some landlord, and it was decided who was a landowner and who was not. The Welsh freemen were held to own their land; the Welsh serfs, the descendants of an old, conquered race, sometimes became owners and sometimes tenants. They all thought that Henry VII, the Welsh victor of Bosworth, had set them free.

4. *The Tudors trusted their people and called upon them to govern and administer justice themselves. The squires were to be justices; the freemen were to be jurors; the shire was to look after the militia, and the parish after the poor."*

Chapter VIII

However, by the time of Henry VIII, England was entering yet another crucial chapter in its history: the Reformation. This was, at the start, a purely political movement in England. Henry VIII wanted to rule over his people the way he wanted, both in religion and politics. Eventually, he became the Supreme Head of the church, as well as the nation's King. With this came new changes. The reformation of the Church was necessary, and Henry VIII was initially tempted to do so due to the enormous wealth of the monasteries. Under the ministry of Thomas Cromwell, however, this Reformation process was hurried on. The monasteries were dissolved (causing a substantial monetary gain to the crown), the Bible was translated, and the influence of Rome was quickly shed off. It was now the King who appointed the bishops, decided on the church cases, and led his country in the direction *he* wanted. How did this pass in Wales? At first, the Welsh were largely indifferent, apathetic even. We must remember that different cultural groups observed this differently: the Irish, for example, saw it as an English movement, and it was thus simply political and could not appeal to the patriots. It was a stark contrast in England, a patriotic, religious, and intellectual movement. Yet in Wales, it was neither welcomed nor opposed: the Welsh tolerated it "with a bad grace."

First and foremost, the Reformation brought English into public worship instead of Latin, which was used up to that point. Latin was venerated but not understood by the commoners. On the other hand, English was understood fully but considered inferior to the ancient Brythonic tongue, the Welsh language. It was also a threat to the Welsh language; if it fell out of use, so would the Welsh identity. It is known that the Tudor dynasty had a great dislike for a variety of languages within the realm. Henry VIII stated, upon giving the Welsh their Act of 1535, that their tongue, the tongue of Owen Tudor (his ancestor), was "nothing like the consonant to the natural mother-tongue used within this realm." Thus he enacted that all officials in Wales "shall speak English." So it happened that the Welsh had all the religious freedom and the promise of salvation: but it was in English, not in Welsh. So, in a way, the Reformation also had its consequences in Wales. Many of the earlier cathedrals, abbeys, churches, relics and religious imagery of Wales were destroyed or taken away by Cromwellian agents. In the end, after all was said and done, the Reformation left Wales poorer and disgruntled.

And, as you might know, the reign of the Tudors had to end at one point. The history of the British Isles in this period is undoubtedly tumultuous and complex, especially with the intertwining of England, Wales, Scotland, and their faiths and cultures. After the Tudors, there came the Stuarts. Where the former did what the people wanted, the latter did what they thought was right; people be damned. New changes came, and those are always hard to accept. Under the Tudor rule, the Crown and the Parliament were in harmony. Queen Elizabeth especially left the people prosperous and instilled a strong view of their rights and religion. However, the Stuart monarchs, such as James I and his son Charles I, both tried to bring changes to law and religion. It now brought a new period of strife. There was significant upheaval in the Parliament from 1603 until 1642. During this time, the Welsh remained fiercely loyal: the Welsh members of the parliament supported the King, and the Welsh people followed the Welsh nobility in their strong loyalty. John Williams arose as a prominent Welshman of this era: he became the Archbishop of York and also Lord Keeper.

Did You Know?

Cantre'r Gwaelod is the mythical submerged land in what is now Cardigan Bay, commonly called the "Welsh Atlantis." It is an alleged sunken kingdom that once stretched across a fertile plain from Bardsey Island to Ramsey Island. This is now Cardigan Bay. Many legends and folk tales exist related to this ancient kingdom and describe various ways it became flooded. A famous story describes Cantre'r Gwaelod as a low-lying land fortified against the sea by a dike, Sarn Badrig ("Saint Patrick's causeway"). This dike had a series of sluice gates that were open at low tide to drain the land. Two princes of this realm held charge over the dike. According to legend, one of these princes, called Seithenyn, is described in one version as a notorious drunkard and carouser, "and it was through his negligence that the sea swept through the open floodgates, ruining the land." Interestingly, even today, at low tide in Cardigan Bay, many remains of ancient, submerged lands and petrified forest remains can be observed: tree stumps, land features, and artificial rock formations.

Eventually, England descended into warfare, and from 1642 until 1646, the First English Civil War raged on. Together with the following conflicts, this period is known as the Wars of the Three Kingdoms or British Civil Wars. It was a war between the Royalists (King's supporters) and the Roundheads (Parliament supporters) and raged across the region, fighting over taxation, religion, freedom, and militia. At this time, Wales remained largely loyal and supported the King. Only the southern part of Pembrokeshire (which had been predominantly English since the time of Henry II) was declared for the Parliament. All this is no strange thing: the King knew how important Wales was to him. Firstly, it could provide him with a powerful Welsh army, which it did on several occasions. It mainly was the Welsh that fought the King's battles: ever since he began his war at Nottingham in 1642, he acquired some 5,000 Welsh warriors at Shrewsbury and marched on London. It was battle after battle, and the poor Welsh infantryman suffered heavily. The Battles of Edgehill, Marston Moor, and Naseby were especially hard and brutal. Sadly, the war spilled over across the borders and into Wales, and no part of the nation was spared.

Prince Rupert and Lord Gerard stood out as the lead Royalist leaders, while Middleton and Michael Jones were the chief Parliament supporters. Although no tremendous or decisive battles were fought in Wales, many skirmishes cost lives. Of course, there was much taking and retaking of towns and castles, and many changed hands repeatedly. It is important to note that Wales had immense strategic importance for the English King, chiefly because it offered two routes to Ireland. For the King, it meant the prospect of the arrival of an Irish army that would guarantee his victory. The port towns of Bristol and Chester, held by the Welsh, were the two ways toward Ireland. The former was taken after a vicious midnight assault, while the latter was eventually forced to yield to the enemy. By March 1647, Harlech Castle was also taken, and the war quickly dwindled to an end, chiefly because the English King was already a prisoner of his enemies.

In an odd turn of events, however, there followed the Second English Civil War, fought between 1648 and 1649, between the two factions of the victorious Parliament. The latter wanted to establish one religion, while the army demanded that every man should worship as he liked. Thus were born the Presbyterian ideal and the Independent ideal. The notorious Cromwell led the army faction, and the Parliament was quickly overwhelmed. What is more, the Presbyterians rose in revolt in Kent, Pembrokeshire, and the lowland areas of Scotland. This resulted in the New Model army marching against the Welsh in war: it was a sure way to sever the connection between the northern and southern Presbyterian supporters. It was in Wales that the future of this second war was to be decided. Cromwell pushed on with ferocity and faced Welsh generals: Laugharne, Powell, and Poyer. All of them fought for the Parliament in the first war. The Welsh leaders were defeated at St. Pagans, near Cardiff, and forced to retreat into Pembroke. In true Welsh warrior fashion, the men decided they would hold out to the last breath within the city's walls. Undaunted, Cromwell besieged them, and thus the siege of Pembroke was the decisive moment of the war.

Pembroke was a formidable castle, one of the strongest in Wales. However, the medieval importance of castles was gone by this time, as gunpowder and cannons were powerful against all fortifications. Unfortunately, Cromwell could not quickly bring all his artillery to the siege; it took time. Thus he was in a difficult position and could not crush the Welsh soldiers as soon as he had hoped. Daily, his challenges mounted, but he stuck it out, as did the Welsh. Once Cromwell had his guns, he hammered the castle walls. After many weeks of siege and several assaults, Pembroke was defeated. Soon after, the war ended: the Scots were also defeated, at the Battle of Preston, while the English King Charles I was tried and sentenced to death. The execution of King Charles I was a great shock in Europe. Amongst the men who signed the king's death warrant were two Welshmen: John Jones of Merioneth and Thomas Wogan of Cardigan, staunch Parliament supporters.

After the Commonwealth was finally established, Wales was viewed with much distrust, especially in the Presbyterian and Royalist areas. Even though Wales was dutifully represented in the Parliament, the representatives were often Englishmen appointed by the government. Wales was under the military dictatorship of major-general Thomas Harrison, who ruled ruthlessly. Still, there were some *honest* attempts to give Wales an efficient clergy. Owen M. Edwards again sums it up succinctly:

"Honest attempts were made to give it an efficient clergy, but the zeal of Vavasour Powel aroused much opposition. Wales either clung tenaciously to its old religion or if it changed it, the changes were extreme. Though the country generally returned to its old life and thought at the Restoration in 1660, much of the new life of the Commonwealth remained: congregations of Independents still met; Quaker ideals survived all

persecution; and even the mysticism of Morgan Lloyd permeated the slowly awakening thought of the peasants whom, in his dreams, he saw welcoming the second advent of Christ."

Next, we go to the 16th, 17th, and 18th centuries. Alas, in the whole history of Wales, these eras might seem the least interesting and a stark contrast to the much more tumultuous English history of that same period. Sadly, this is often the case in Welsh history books. Many simply stop around 1284 or skim over the few crucial rebellions until the mid-1500s. Moreover, in the broader history of the British Isles, the Welsh are merely displayed as law-abiding and loyal folk, and their general history is simply skipped. This is done due to a sad but simple fact: the overall flow of Welsh history is simply the gradual dwindling and disappearance of independent Welsh institutions. When the English King was brought back to the throne in the Restoration in 1660, so was the Court of Wales. However, its work was done, and by 1689 it ended.

Throughout the 18th century, sadly, the Welsh church suffered many cases of abuse. Administered from England, it was incredibly out of touch with the Welsh people. Under the English Hanoverian Kings, the bishoprics of Wales were regarded as rewards for public service and steppingstones toward more lucrative appointments in England. Even sadder is that from 1713 until 1870, no bishop could preach in the Welsh language. This all displayed a remarkable lack of interest in Welsh affairs on the part of the Church. These abuses, combined with the tremendous educational advance of the people, caused great distress in Wales and were fertile ground for debate and religious revival. This revival started in the 1730s and was led by a noted Breconshire layman, Howell Harris, and Daniel Rowland, a curate from Cardiganshire. Their movement was independent but quite similar to the "great crusade of evangelical preaching" that was started contemporaneously in England by John and Charles Wesley and George Whitefield, the so-called "Methodists." Like their English counterparts, Harris and his followers did not intend to start a separate denomination but to restore the Church to its original spiritual mission. Because of this, they were not originally dissenters like the Quakers, Baptists, and Independents were.

Through the movement of Howell Harris, one noted disciple arose: William Williams, also known as William Pantycelyn. He was one of the earliest adherents of Harris and rose as a preacher and writer of over 800 hymns. His glorious hymns and other religious poems and prose he wrote quickly became a fundamental part of Welsh national literature. Of course, the poetic and emotional hymns were quick to win over the disaffected Welsh people. This poignant way of Methodist preaching gained many converts. From the early days, the movement was based in the south of Wales, but by the 1780s, it carried over to the north, primarily through the work of Thomas Charles, an Anglican parson, from the settlement of Baya. Thomas Charles was one of the founders of the British and Foreign Bible Society and was the man who introduced Sunday School as well. Like the early Methodist leaders, Thomas Charles did not want to break off with the Church. Driven by the pressure from his followers and the Church's opposition, he ultimately took a final step in the rupture of 1811 by ordaining Methodist ministers. Even before this happened, in 1742, Wesley and Whitefield, whom we mentioned before, disagreed greatly on the matter of Predestination. In the end, Harris and the other Welsh Methodists adopted the doctrine of Whitefield and thus became Calvinistic Methodists. It took nearly 200 years before these Methodist sects would unite in 1932. They became the Methodist Church, but the only church of purely Welsh origins, the Calvinistic Methodist Church of Wales, remained separate.

The following year, the Calvinistic Methodist Church of Wales gained autonomy in spiritual matters by the 1933 Act of Parliament. It should not come as a surprise to know that the adherents of these movements came primarily from poorer farming and laboring classes.

In stark contrast, the nobles and the gentry remained staunch Anglicans and thus became separate in speech and religion from most Welsh people. After a while, about 80% of the Welsh were adherents of Nonconformist religions, mostly Methodism. In many ways, the spread of Methodism and similar Nonconformist doctrines affected moral life in Wales. People became more sober and severe according to their religious views. A wonderful thing came about: the revival of interest in Welsh traditions and culture. In 1751, Welshmen in London founded The Honourable Society of Cymmrodorion, a movement "for the encouragement of literature, science, and art as connected with Wales." Another great thing followed: the National Eisteddfod of Wales event was brought back to life in 1789, after a gap of more than two hundred years.

Chapter IX

The cultural and religious revivals were thus the two main currents of Welsh history in the period of a hundred years between the middle of the 18th and the middle of the 19th centuries. The third primary current of this period of Welsh history was, of course, the Industrial Revolution. Ever since the 16th century, substantial mining has been conducted in Wales. As we mentioned, Wales was a significant source of coal, slate, iron, and other ores. Thus it had an extensive mining background. The most productive were lead mines in Cardiganshire and Flintshire. From the 1740s onwards, these mining operations were turned into large-scale undertakings, primarily to fuel the many wars that began. From then on, Glamorgan's coal fields became the biggest ore producers and a center of activity. In 1759, on the northern edge of the coal fields, near the hamlet of Merthyr Tydfil, the iron industry began and quickly gained in speed. The town became one of the regional centers of the iron industry. Until the 1830s (when smokeless coal was discovered in the Aberdare district), coal mining was, in fact, subsidiary to the production of iron. By 1800 Merthyr Tydfil boasted a population of 7,000 and was one of the largest towns in Wales. However, its sudden expansion caused it to suffer many drawbacks that other large industrial towns of the time had. It was unsanitary, full of slums, surrounded by slag heaps, and had a large population of poor citizens. Many diseases broke out in its most impoverished slums.

The other chief development of the mid-18th century was rediscovering large quantities of copper ore that could be easily mined. It was located on the Parys Mountain in Anglesey and had been working since Roman times. From the 1760s until the early 1800s, Anglesey had a brief but significant period of predominance in world copper mining. In the near modern period, Wales excelled as one of the principal mining nations in Europe, if not the world.

Wales excelled in copper and coal production: from the 1830s, coal production was surplus to the needs of the local industries. It had good quality and was thus exported to London and Paris. Of course, this led to the development of railroad industries, which allowed the ore to be moved to the ports for export in large quantities and quickly. This led to the expansion of Cardiff, the chief port centered on this trade. Today it is the capital of Wales. It started as a small market town with less than 2,000 citizens, and by 1850 it boasted a population of nearly 20,000. Still, at this time, Merthyr Tydfil was the largest Welsh town with almost 50,000 citizens (later to be significantly reduced), and Swansea had about 30,000. As we mentioned, slate quarrying was the chief industry of the north of Wales. In Northern Caernarvonshire were the Penrhyn quarries, developed between 1780 and 1820 by Richard Pennant, Baron Penrhyn. The quarry became a slate producer of world renown, and by 1850 the quarrying of slate was the basis of the economy of North Wales. It was said that the Welsh slate was of the best quality in the world.

Wales's population doubled in the first half of the 19th century with the booming industry and the great expansion of railways. It grew from about 600,000 to nearly 1,200,000. Many citizens of rural populations went over into the ever-expanding mines and quarries to try their luck there. In 1800, Wales was recorded as being three-quarters rural, but in 1850, it was reduced to just two-thirds. Moreover, even people from England, Cornwall, and Ireland crossed over to Wales to try their luck in the mines and quarries, especially in the south, where the population increase was the greatest, as was the industry. However, almost all of the workers in the northern quarries were Welsh. As you can imagine, the hard and heavy industry in those times was far from perfect and had deplorable conditions. The emergence of an industrial working class that lived under terrible conditions, as well as the rise of an economic depression that followed the Napoleonic Wars, added to the over-population in rural areas and the political grievances, all helped create the rise of social unrest during the second quarter of the 19th century. This led to several industrial strikes in the north and the south. However, they had no organization and were thus quickly abandoned.

Trade Unions spread into Wales from England in the 1830s, but it took a while until they were established there. The inhabitants of the rural districts suffered great poverty, and the rise of distress led to the infamous Rebecca riots from 1839 until 1843. During these riots, angry mobs made up of tenant farmers were disguised as women. These overburdened farmers were protesting the heavy tolls they were being charged for using the roads levied by the businessmen who owned them. The female-clad farmers destroyed the turnpike gates. The name "Rebecca" was adopted by the riot leaders and was taken from a scriptural blessing found in the 24th chapter of Genesis, verse 60, which reads: "They blessed Rebekah and said to her ... may your descendants possess the gate of those who hate them." The riots were great and required the deployment of troops to be suppressed. Politics and legislation eventually removed most of the grievances made by the folk.

"Agitation for political reform began with the Non-conformist middle classes, mainly the older Dissenting sects, who embraced the new Radicalism of the extreme Liberals of England. Most of them were, however, averse to the use of force, and the Methodists, who felt that interference with the supposed Divine Will would be sinful, remained politically passive."

Some much-needed changes were delivered with the Reform Act of 1832. Through this act, many so-called "rotten boroughs" were finally abolished, and seats were given to the larger towns. The franchise was extended, but less than one in twenty had the vote. More changes were needed. Thus, more agitation for further reforms was started by the so-called "Chartists." They thought their six-point People's Charter for parliamentary reform, which included universal male suffrage, would end all their problems and great poverty. The movement affected the middle and lower classes. Eventually, it spread across Wales, especially into Montgomeryshire, where the unemployed were in great numbers due to the slump in the old woolen industry. In time, Monmouthshire became the center of the movement. The Chartists organized petitions and massive demonstrations. The largest demonstration in Wales was in Newport in 1839, but it was quickly quelled, and its leaders were transported to penal colonies. After this year, the Chartist movement lost momentum and dwindled until 1848, when it was finally gone. Afterward, the Welsh working classes turned their attention toward creating their trade union movement.

In 1847 the government published its report of an inquiry into the state of education in Wales. This report drew the people's attention to many critical shortcomings in the system and even went further. It shows a strong anti-Nonconformist (majority of Welsh) bias and even went so far as to regard the survival of the Welsh language as a great evil. This caused the (until then) passive Methodists to react. In their

Sunday Schools, after all, Welsh was taught as a basis for scriptural study. From that point on, Radicalism became "the creed" for Welsh Dissenters, and Nonconformists Liberals began to pursue seats in the Parliament, which was up to that point a "preserve" for the Anglican gentry. It was a significant change for the Welsh people and an important milestone in the history of Wales.

In the second half of the 19th century, the coal industry of South Wales experienced another vast expansion. This was spurred by the rapid growth of railways and the gradual transition from classic sail ships to steam-powered ones. These changes created new demands at home and abroad, and exports boomed. In particular, demand was the high-quality coal from the Rhondda Valley. By the end of the century, the Navy relied on Welsh coal exclusively, and the export of coal from Cardiff port rose to a staggering ten million tons a year, making Wales a coal-producing giant. As a result, the population of Cardiff rose from a meager 18,000 in 1851 to a staggering 164,000 in 1901, just fifty years later. This made it the largest town in Wales at that point, by far. Other towns boomed also. Swansea was a great port and a center of the tin-plate industry. By 1875, three-quarters of British tin-plate production came from South Wales and Swansea. The steel and iron industries flourished but were overshadowed by coal production. Copper smelting persevered until about 1890, when foreign competition caused it to decline considerably. Of course, it would be silly to say that only South Wales boasted a flourishing industry. Industrial development was underway in northeast Wales as well, in Denbighshire, the place of the North Wales coalfields, and in Flintshire. However, those traditional and older Welsh industries began to dwindle. These were lead mines and slate quarries: the former was exhausted by 1870, while the latter suffered in the 1880s from foreign competitors. Those famous Penrhyn slate quarries, which we mentioned before, were devastated by a year-long strike between 1896 and 1897, then again in 1900, lasting for three years.

As before, the population of Wales continued to rise steadily. All this was the direct result of its massive industrial expansion. From 1851 until 1911, the country's population doubled in just sixty years. From some 1,200,000, it rose to 2,500,000, and the vast majority of that increase was centered on urban areas. This created a significant change in Wales: in 1851, the nation was two-thirds rural, but in 1911 it was two-thirds urban. It needs to be taken into account that a contributing factor to the remarkable rise in population was also the influx of Englishmen into the areas of Glamorgan and Monmouthshire.

Chapter X

In terms of politics, there were large-scale changes, too. Yes, we know politics can be somewhat tedious to read about, but they are undoubtedly a crucial aspect of the history of every nation, Wales especially. The rise of new Welsh political parties was a big thing that would change the flow of Welsh history. So it was that on the political front, the challenge of the Nonconformist Liberals for the seats in the Parliament achieved an important success. This party won a meaningful victory in the General Election of 1868 and gained about two-thirds of the Welsh seats in the parliament. This was the direct result of the extension of the franchise in 1867 to those classes where Nonconformist beliefs were strong. Through this election, William Ewart Gladstone was also brought to power. Gladstone acquired a significant following among the nonconformists, mainly because he tended to regard all big political questions as moral issues. He was loved by the commoners and gained a popular nickname, "The People's William." The swing to the Liberals continued after this, and in the 1885 Election, they gained 30 out of 34 Welsh seats. Towards the century's end, organized trade unionism began to take over the leadership of the industrial areas from the middle-class liberals. Miner strikes continued: notable was the strike at Penrhyn slate quarries and a miner's strike of 1898, which caused a six-month stoppage in half the pits of South Wales. In 1900 the Scottish ex-miner Keir Hardie was elected and became the chief founder of the Independent Labor Party of Great Britain. He became the first Labor Member of the Parliament. Furthermore, the strength of the Labor Party in Parliament continued to grow from 2 in 1900 to 42 in 1910. Six represented Welsh constituencies (out of 34 total Welsh seats).

Through politics undeniably comes patriotism. The Welsh radicalism that arose in the second half of the 19th century quickly grew into a form of political nationalism. As we mentioned, the revival of Welsh national feeling and identity began some hundred years earlier and was spurred by the London-based Cymmrodorion Society. Until this point, it was confined only to cultural affairs; however, from the 1850s onwards, politics greatly influenced it. Furthermore, the London-based Liberation Society aimed to separate Church and State and set up its branches in Wales.

In Wales, there was a traditional opposition to the dominance of the Welsh Church by the Church of England, and now the chief goal of Nonconformist Radicalism was the disestablishment of the Welsh Church. The political "cleavage" was between the mainly conservative, English-speaking, and Anglican gentry on one side and the Liberal, Welsh-speaking Nationalistic Conformists on the other. One of the interesting "off-shoots" of this new wave of Welsh nationalism was migration, mostly under the leadership of the Nonconformists. This migration was into the Patagonia region of Argentina, in South America. It was done in coordination with the Argentinian Government, which wanted to settle the uninhabited areas of Patagonia. From the mid-1800s, several hundred Welsh immigrants sailed across the oceans searching for a new start in Patagonia. The start was precarious and rife with difficulties. Eventually, the folk soon mastered this new land and established several Welsh towns in a region they named *Y Wladfa*. Even today, these towns are proud of their Welsh heritage, and they are not assimilated. Many still speak Welsh, besides Spanish.

Now, let us return to the politics of near-modern Wales. In the 1880s, the Nationalistic movement reached its peak. William Ewart Gladstone favored Welsh aspirations and soon became the hero of Welsh Nonconformists. He was also the largest landlord in the area of Flintshire at that time. In 1885, the Welsh Liberals formed a Welsh Parliamentary Party and exerted critical influence. The following year, they started the Young Wales (Cymru Fydd) movement aimed at home rule for Wales. The leader of this movement was Thomas Ellis, a son of a Merioneth Methodist farmer. Later, Ellis was joined by the newly elected Liberal Member for Caernarvon in 1890, young David Lloyd George. When the two of them took Government Office, the Cymru Fydd movement collapsed, and from 1895 the Welsh political nationalism fell into abeyance until it was eventually revived in 1925.

More importantly, the nationalist movement also successfully established a largely autonomous education system in Wales, from elementary schools to universities. In 1872, the College at Aberystwyth was founded but was supported by voluntary contributions. State-aided University Colleges were established, first in Cardiff in 1883 and then in Bangor in 1884. In 1893, these three institutions were combined to form the University of Wales. For the Welsh people, this was an important event. State-aided secondary schools were also started. In 1907, the Welsh Department of the Board of Education was created. With that, the teaching of Welsh was finally accepted. In 1920 the fourth college from Swansea was added. One sad fact remains, however, the gradual decline of the use of the Welsh language.

Even though educational encouragement was given to the Welsh language, its use decreased simply because advancement often depended solely on fluency in English. The typical, non-patriotic student thought, why learn Welsh if it is of no use? So, in 1901, just half of the Welsh population could speak Welsh. Twenty years later, in 1921, Welsh speakers were a third of the total population. In modern times, according to the Welsh Language Use Survey of 2019-20, some 48% of Welsh speakers considered themselves fluent in Welsh. Even though the numbers declined in the 1900s, the revival of Welsh culture continued steadily. The National Eisteddfod, a big event for the Welsh, became an annual event in 1880 and primarily promoted Welsh culture. In the early 20th century, the National Museum at Cardiff was opened, as was the National Library at Aberystwyth. Both served to bring the Welsh identity closer to the average Welsh person.

In the early years of the 20th century, Wales as a whole had a heavy aspect of pacifism. This was spurred by the politician Lloyd George's disapproval of the Boer War, a hot topic at the time. However, that pacifist current could not endure the great trouble of the 1900s, the First World War. No country in Europe was spared the bloodshed, Wales included. When the war erupted in 1914, Wales answered the call of duty in its noblest fashion. By the end of 1915, there were 50,000 Welsh in the armed forces. During the war, the Welsh regiments raised nearly a hundred battalions combined.

Did You Know?

David Lloyd George was one of the prominent Welsh-born politicians of the United Kingdom. He was born in Manchester in 1863, a son of a Welsh schoolmaster. He was brought up in a village near Criccieth in Caernarvonshire and went to the village school. Later in his life, he became a solicitor and embraced the rising Cymru Fydd (Young Wales) Movement. He was elected the M.P. for Caernarvonshire in 1890. Soon he rose to prominence. He was described as having great personal charm and eloquence and the emotionalism and enthusiasm of the Welsh Nonconformists. Subsequently, he became the most distinguished statesman of Welsh origins and gained enduring fame for leading Britain in the First World War as Prime Minister from 1916 until 1922. Before he became the Prime Minister, he held several important Government positions. From 1922 and on, Lloyd George never held office. Until 1931 he strove to reunite and revive the Liberal party.

These regiments were: The Royal Welsh Fusiliers, the Welsh Guards, The Welsh Regiment, and the South Wales Borderers. Sadly, many young lives were lost in this bloody and devastating war. However, it also brought an economic boom and a vast expansion of heavy industry and agriculture in Wales. However, this was an "artificial prosperity," and it collapsed soon after the war ended. The Welsh economy of the time depended solely on three things: coal, steel, and tin-plate, and the export market for these goods. However, this market dwindled soon after the war. Unemployment soared. Agriculture also required less labor with each passing year. By the early 1930s, the unemployed numbered a quarter of a million. That same number previously migrated to England in search of work. The government took action, as did private enterprises. They brought new industries to South Wales and gradually alleviated the problematic situation. Again, from these hardships, the economic depression, and the unwelcome changes in employment and way of life, the Welsh people sought comfort in their own identity and culture, leading to another wave of interest in Welsh culture and nationalism. Of course, from this new era, politics were changed too. The Labor Party was now backed by highly organized trade unions and held a dominant position in Welsh politics. It meant that Nonconformist Liberalism, after nearly 50 years of political leadership in Wales, was now down to only a few seats in the Parliament.

In 1922, the Welsh League of Youth was founded, and it aimed to stop the drift away from the Welsh language. After its formation in 1927, the Board of Education produced a bilingual teaching program in schools, a crucial milestone for preserving the Welsh language with ancient roots. However, the success was moderate, and some separation from Welsh still existed. In 1925 the Plaid Cymru was formed, the Welsh National Party, which strove to revive nationalism and to create a separate Welsh Parliament. It gained support mainly from the poorer rural districts. It should not come as a surprise that the ambitions of Plaid Cymru were spurred by the neighboring Irish, who obtained Dominion status as the Irish Free State. However, Plaid Cymru only achieved some success after the end of World War Two. This terrible conflict, which again swept over Europe, dragged off young Welsh into the chaos of war. Even so, the war brought, once more, full employment into Wales, as the war effort fired up the heavy industries. However, the war also threatened the old and traditional Welsh way of life. The rural areas received an influx of civilians and evacuees from English cities, and the wartime restrictions on crowds and travel limited the traditional Eisteddfod activities. Again, just as in the Great War, the economic boom began declining after the war ended. The demand for slate and coal declined, quarries and mines were closed, and even less labor was required in agriculture and industry, especially with the advent of new machines and technologies. All this created mass discontent and hardships; through these, the Welsh people demanded more Welsh Control of the local affairs. The nationalist movement Plaid Cymru gained even more support. Demonstrations and protests were expected. In 1955 Cardiff was granted the status of "capital," which met some of the Welsh aspirations. The Welsh Office in Cardiff controls many aspects of Welsh life. Also, in these post-war years, the Welsh language was backed by the broadcasting of Welsh stations on radio and TV, which put out programs in Welsh only, and in English. Sadly, the number of Welsh speakers is still in decline, even today. In 1921 there were over 600,000 of them, and in 1961, only 656,000. Of these, only 26,000 exclusively spoke Welsh and had no English.

The total population of Wales remained relatively static over these years, with no significant shifts. Migrations balanced out the natural increase in the search for work. Just like the English, the Scottish, and the Irish, Welsh people also sailed across the oceans in search of a better future. They settled in the cities of America and Canada, creating a Welsh diaspora there. There were considerable numbers of Welsh in Canada, New Zealand, Australia, America, and elsewhere.

Conclusion

"There is one other characteristic of modern Wales—a certain pride, not so much in what has been done, but in what is going to be done. Wales is small, though not much smaller than Palestine, Holland, or Switzerland, and every part of it knows the other. There is a healthy rivalry between its towns and between its colleges; each town can show that it has done something for Wales in the past by means of its industries, or school, or press. In the strong feeling of unity, there is ambition to surpass, and each part lives in the light of the action of the other parts. The day is a day of incessant activity, industrial, educational, literary, and political. What is true in the life of the individual is true in the life of a nation: a day of hard work is a happy day and a day of hope."

So writes Sir Owen Morgan Edwards in his History of Wales. It is a perfect, poignant summary of an ancient and proud nation that never lost its hope. Wales is a nation from whose history we can learn so much. One glance is enough to tell us of endless perseverance, of stubborn defiance despite all. Throughout the centuries, Wales stood its ground in the face of invaders and oppressive overlords. It held on dearly to its unique identity and culture, knowing far too well that Wales would be no more without them. From the ancient Brythonic realms, which stood in the face of the Anglo-Saxons and the Vikings, down to the pressures of the Normans and the later English Kingdom, Wales fought on and could not be erased. This nation of ancient Britons shared a hard fate with neighboring Cornwall, the northern kingdoms of Hen Ogledd, with their neighbors from Ireland and Scotland: they all suffered at the hands of great English kings and their endless aspirations. Even so, the Welsh kept their name, language, culture, and ancient identity through hard work and defiance. And with them safe, they remained a unique people in the British Isles, thoroughly different from their neighbors. Today, Wales is a country that is a valuable part of the United Kingdom. Its language is still very much alive, although it could benefit from more speakers. It is a land of a stable economy, infrastructure, prosperity, and living culture. The natural *eisteddfod* competitions are alive and well and keep the oldest Welsh traditions moving. Although relatively small, Wales is packed to the brim with many natural wonders, fantastic sceneries, protected areas, archeological sites, and ancient relics. It boasts hundreds of castles and castle ruins, a relic of its tumultuous medieval history, and it is also dotted with many very ancient dolmens and megalithic structures. One could spend decades traveling across Wales and assisting all these sites, learning so much. The land is packed with wonders, from Anglesey in the North to Swansea in the South. All this is due to the vibrant, rich, and sometimes arduous history of Wales.

References:

Breverton, T. 2009. *Wales: A Historical Companion.* Amberley Publishing Limited.

Charles-Edwards, T. M. 2013. *Wales and the Britons, 350-1064.* OUP Oxford.

Davies, R. R. 2000. *The Age of Conquest: Wales, 1063-1415.* Oxford University Press.

Davies, R. 2015. *People, Places and Passions: A Social History of Wales and the Welsh.* University of Wales Press.

Davies, R. R. 2009. *Owain Glyndwr: Prince of Wales.* Y Lolfa.

Davies, S. 2004. *War And Society In Medieval Wales, 633–1283. Welsh Military Institutions.* University of Wales Press.

Edwards, M. O. 2018. *A Short History of Wales.* BoD - Books on Demand.

Jameson, O. *A Short History of Wales.* Stanford.

Jenkins, H. G. 2007. *A Concise History of Wales.* Cambridge University Press.

Jenkins, P. 2014. *A History of Modern Wales 1536-1990.* Routledge.

Jones, G. J. 2014. *The History of Wales.* University of Wales Press.

Jones, G. E. 1994. *Modern Wales: A Concise History.* Cambridge University Press.

Stephenson, D. 2019. *Medieval Wales c .1050–1332: Centuries of Ambiguity.* University of Wales Press.

Don't miss out!

Visit the website below and you can sign up to receive emails whenever History Nerds publishes a new book. There's no charge and no obligation.

https://books2read.com/r/B-A-ODOK-SDPAC

BOOKS 2 READ

Connecting independent readers to independent writers.

Also by History Nerds

Celtic History
Ireland

Great Wars of the World
World War 1
World War 2
The Napoleonic Wars: One Shot at Glory
The Serbian Revolution: 1804-1835
Peace Won by the Saber: The Crimean War, 1853-1856
The Wars of the Roses

Irish Heroes
Grace O'Malley: The Pirate Queen of Ireland
William Butler Yeats: Nobel Prize Winning Poet
Scáthach
Finn McCool

The History of the Vikings

Vikings
Longships on Restless Seas

The Rise and Fall of Empires
Rome: The Rise and Fall

Standalone
The History of the United Kingdom
The History of Ireland
The History of America
Stalin
The Fiery Maelstrom of Freedom
The History of Scotland
Robert the Bruce
William Wallace: Scotland's Great Freedom Fighter
The History of Wales

9 7 9 8 2 1 5 9 8 5 7 0 0